Presented to

_____

by

_____

On the Occasion of

_____

Date

_____

The Presence of God is life's highest goal for the believer. Here is a book that will aid any sincere Christian in attaining that goal. Rebecca Barlow Jordan has given us a practical and inspiring volume on that subject, and I highly recommend it to anyone who would seek God's daily Presence.

LEWIS A. DRUMMOND
Billy Graham Professor of Evangelism
Samford University

Reading *Daily in Your Presence* is like walking through a soft, refreshing early morning rain. I experienced God's love washing over me, His hand gently guiding me, and His principles providing renewed perspectives on everyday activities. This is a book I will treasure personally and a gift I will purchase for my friends.

CAROL KENT, PRESIDENT
Speak Up Speaker Services
International Speaker and Author

Rebecca Jordan has enjoyed intimate conversations with a loving Father. Now, she helps others sample the transforming experience firsthand. Rebecca's insights evolve from her firsthand experience and help us receive the penetrating truth that we have a truly loving Father who has much to tell us.

DR. DEBORAH NEWMAN
Author, Counselor

For several years I have been fascinated by the seemingly limitless names for our Father that I've found in God's Word. It was with delight, then, that I found *Daily in Your Presence*. Rebecca Barlow Jordan leads the reader daily to a new insight about the character of God, and I recommend her book to those who are yearning for a more intimate relationship with Him.

Rebecca Barlow Jordan has written a series of touching and tender colloquies that lead the reader deeper into the Abba experience.

I love the format of Rebecca's new book. Words from the Father's Heart to the reader's heart, then time to reflect, which we all need. My favorite part is Simple Truth. This short statement is worth pondering and writing down, so your life can internalize the simple truth. Another winner by Becky!

Rebecca Jordan's *Daily In Your Presence* gently leads the reader through a deeper understanding of God's character and offers an open door to freshly experiencing His love for her personally.

DAILY IN YOUR PRESENCE

Intimate Conversations with a Loving Father

REBECCA BARLOW JORDAN

BARBOUR
PUBLISHING

DAILY IN YOUR PRESENCE

Published by Barbour Publishing, Inc., P.O. Box 719, Uhrichsville, Ohio 44683, www.barbourbooks.com

Our mission is to publish and distribute inspirational products offering exceptional value and biblical encouragement to the masses.

 Member of the
Evangelical Christian
Publishers Association

Printed in the United States of America.
5 4

Dedication

To the Name above all names,
the One who is worthy of all my praise.
Oh, for a thousand ways and more
To praise my loving Lord,
That I might give Him thanks each day
From the depths of a grateful heart.

REBECCA BARLOW JORDAN

Special Thanks

To the editorial, marketing, and sales teams of Barbour Publishing, Inc., and for all the work that goes on behind the scenes that only they know about—many thanks!

To my husband, Larry, who keeps letting me write my heart, and who inspires me to seek my Father's heart daily, you are a permanent part of my heart!

To those who prayed for me during the writing of this book—family members, friends, church members, my Bible study class, and the women of my support team, Ruth, Priscilla, Sharon, and Mary—your prayers and encouragement made the difference (especially during computer glitches).

To my precious heavenly Father whose love, grace, and faithfulness never cease to amaze me—with deep gratitude for allowing me the joy of His intimate conversations and daily presence.

Introduction

What do you say to the God of the universe? How do you approach the Lord of hosts? Why would the King of kings want to spend time with a lowly servant? Can I really expect God to be my Father? To sit down and talk as an intimate friend? What does it mean to be His child? Does Jesus really, really love me and accept me as I am? What does He expect from me? Does He care? Why would a holy God want to fellowship with me anyway?

If you've ever asked yourself even one of those questions, this book is for you. In *At Home in My Heart, Preparing a Place for His Presence,* I invited you to take a tour with me as Jesus renovated my heart and home. I hope you invited Him to walk through yours, as well. The tour is complete, for now, though Jesus is always at work—in my heart and in yours—conforming, correcting, and celebrating His own creation. Now it's time to rest a while. Will you pull up a chair by the fire and join me once again as we celebrate the work and character of an awesome God?

In this book it was not my intention to try to bring God down to our level or to lift us up to His. Through His grace and mercy, Jesus already did that. These prayer conversations are short and simple. If you do nothing but meditate daily on the names and attributes of God, offering a prayer of thanks and praise for His character, you will be blessed. In fact, I encourage you to review all the names at least once a month with a prayer that simply says, "Praise You, God, for being my _____ [then add the names or attributes you read]." As I researched His names and spent time meditating on His beautiful character, there were times when I had to stop typing. His love, grace, and comfort so overwhelmed me, tears of gratitude flowed freely. Crying out, "Abba! Daddy!" or "Holy, Holy, Holy," I entered the awesome joy of His presence as I hope you will. If you allow Him, the powerful name of the Almighty will change your countenance, actions, and reactions. He will bring comfort, assurance, strength, and joy as only a Father can.

God desires your fellowship—even more than you desire His. He wants to converse with you, as a loving Father with His child. Come, and enter the intimate presence of the Lord. As you take a few moments each day to join Him in simple conversation, feel free to kneel, shout, pray, sing, cry, or bow in silence. Stay as long as you wish. I hope when your time together is finished, your heart will be strangely warmed like mine. And I hope that this year will be the start of many more intimate conversations with a loving Father. Enjoy His presence!

REBECCA

ALPHA AND OMEGA

*"I am the Alpha and the Omega,
the Beginning and the End."*

REVELATION 21:6

FROM THE FATHER'S HEART

My child, you are often confused about who I am and where you are going. When you arise in the morning, I am there with you. When you work through the day, you will find Me close by. From the time you open your eyes until I close them in sleep at night, I am always with you, ready to guide you. Do not worry about knowing how you fit into My plans. Be concerned only with knowing Me and spending time together. Your future is in My hands.

A GRATEFUL RESPONSE

In Your time, Lord, every step is ordered and every thought recorded. You know the past, present, and future. You have planned every day of my life with purpose and love.

Gently but firmly You are preparing a glorious ending for me in heaven. I give my life into Your safekeeping. How marvelous is Your wisdom!

SIMPLE TRUTH

Life is a journey that begins and ends with God.

BRANCH

*In that day the Branch of the LORD
will be beautiful and glorious.*

ISAIAH 4:2

FROM THE FATHER'S HEART

My child, I've heard your cries and protests. When the heat is turned up, My love rises even higher. Do you not know I see and hear the injustices you feel? Do you not realize I am providing for you even in the moments of your greatest frustrations? No matter where you go, I will cover you with My comforting grace.

A GRATEFUL RESPONSE

Lord, You are a towering branch that protects me from the sweltering heat of oppression. Hovering over me, You shelter me with the shade of Your Spirit each day. I have felt the refreshing breath of Your presence, and I am grateful for the sweetness of Your comfort. O Lord, how beautiful is Your name!

SIMPLE TRUTH

*God's mercies never dry up. His "branches" will
always reach far enough to cover us.*

Day 3

FAITHFULNESS

*The LORD is faithful to all his promises
and loving toward all he has made.*

PSALM 145:13

FROM THE FATHER'S HEART

My child, because you are anxious about so many things, I want you to look to My Word for assurance. Remember how I fulfilled every promise I made. Look at My servants Abraham, Isaac, Ruth, David, and a host of mighty men and women throughout Scripture. I love you, too, just as I loved them. As I was faithful to My covenant with them, so I will be faithful to you. I always keep My Word.

A GRATEFUL RESPONSE

As I look back over my life, Lord, I see the tracks of Your faithfulness. Sometimes carrying me, sometimes walking beside me, You are always the same. Time after time, even when I fail You, Lord, Your promises remain. You are always true to Your Word.

Great is Your faithfulness.

SIMPLE TRUTH

It is impossible for God to break His promises. He and His Word are the same.

Day 4

CREATOR

*The LORD is the everlasting God,
the Creator of the ends of the earth.*

ISAIAH 40:28

FROM THE FATHER'S HEART

My child, when your thoughts are filled with the ugliness of the world, remember it is not I who erased the beauty. I splashed the parched ground with paint drops of color. I nestled my creatures safely together like clustered jewels and carved out a home for each one. Every day is a personalized tapestry of love from Me to you. From the beginning, I planted My beauty in your heart so you could see life through My eyes. Those who cannot acknowledge the glory of My creation will not recognize Me.

A GRATEFUL RESPONSE

From the splendor of mountain majesty to the simplicity of desert plain, I see Your hand at work, Lord—a heavenly original. All Your creatures show the uniqueness of Your glory, the pride of Your handiwork, and the tenderness of Your love. Thank You for beauty, Lord.

SIMPLE TRUTH

God loves for us to celebrate with Him the finished work of His own hands: "It is good! It is good! It is good!"

WONDERFUL COUNSELOR

And he will be called
Wonderful Counselor.

ISAIAH 9:6

FROM THE FATHER'S HEART

My child, I see your confused and hurting heart. You are facing a mountain of decisions, yet you feel paralyzed and helpless to act. I am always ready to counsel you, not with chiding words or accusing fingers but with arms of love. Rest in Me a while, and soon you will see the clouds disappear. I will put My thoughts within you to help you make wise choices. Trust Me today.

A GRATEFUL RESPONSE

Amid the hurt, joy, and unanswered questions, You are there with listening ears and compassionate eyes. With discerning thought and gentle affirmation, You speak directly to the issues of my life. No one but You knows how the patterns of my life fit together.

Thank You, Lord, for always being there.

SIMPLE TRUTH

God is never the author of confusion. His counsel is
100 percent accurate.

COMPASSION

His compassions never fail.
They are new every morning; great is your faithfulness.

LAMENTATIONS 3:22–23

FROM THE FATHER'S HEART

My child, are you struggling with failure? My compassion has no end. While I will not compromise My plan for obedience, I am not deaf to your cries for help. What you see as the point of no return, I see as the possibility of a new beginning. I have no desire to destroy you or My dreams for you. Like a father loves his child, I, too, love you. Rest in Me daily, and let Me demonstrate My love and compassion to you.

A GRATEFUL RESPONSE

No matter what I did yesterday, You stand before me each new morning with outstretched arms, inviting me to start over. You see me not as I was, but as I am becoming. Your compassion overwhelms me and draws me even closer to You, Lord.

SIMPLE TRUTH

God's plan is never destruction, only restoration.

REFUGE

God is our refuge and strength,
an ever-present help in trouble.

PSALM 46:1

FROM THE FATHER'S HEART

My child, sit down in the boat. Don't look at the billowing waves or the sea spewing its anger in all directions. I made the wind and the sea; they listen and obey My voice. I walk on the clouds, and they thunder their praise. I blink My eyes, and lightning reflects My power. I hold out My hand, and the storms are stilled. So, take My hand, sit down, and relax. Do you think the God who knows the number of hairs on your head will abandon you in your greatest hour of need? Be still, My child. You are safe with Me.

A GRATEFUL RESPONSE

When the storms rage around me, I can always run to You and rest, Lord. In turbulent times, in trials and temptations, in weakness or in fear, You are my strength, and Your hiding place is secure. Bless You, Lord, for being my refuge.

SIMPLE TRUTH

If God does not rescue us immediately, it is only
because He has a greater purpose in mind. He will
still give us peace in the center of our storms.

GOOD SHEPHERD

"I am the good shepherd;
I know my sheep and my sheep know me."

JOHN 10:14

FROM THE FATHER'S HEART

My child, you may think you know where the pastures are greener. At times you may even try to sneak under the fence or walk another path. But as your good shepherd, I know your name. And I will never stop looking for you and calling you back. You may not understand My reason for boundaries, but the gate is there to protect you. I will feed you with nourishing food—not just for your body, but for your soul. I will give you rest, refreshment, and joy for your journey. Stay close, because I am all you need.

A GRATEFUL RESPONSE

Wherever I go—up steep mountain paths, through the deep valleys and green pastures, or around still waters—You walk beside me, refreshing my spirit and restoring my soul. If I stray, You pursue me until I can rest safely in Your arms again. What a wonderful shepherd You are!

SIMPLE TRUTH

You can't hear the shepherd's voice if you're always following the wrong sheep.

DAILY IN YOUR PRESENCE

FORGIVENESS

*"For I will forgive their wickedness
and will remember their sins no more."*

JEREMIAH 31:34

FROM THE FATHER'S HEART

My child, of course I know your past. Why do you wrestle with something that I so long ago forgave? My death paid for your wrong actions and attitudes. The "books" are now balanced. I no longer hold you accountable for what you did in the past. You are forgiven. Now let Me fill those clean pages with a future that I have designed especially for you. Hold your head up, but keep your heart bowed before Me. Together, let's press on to the prize for which I have called you.

A GRATEFUL RESPONSE

Lord, the past is gone, and I must leave it behind. Although I remember my sins well, You have thrown them into the sea of forgetfulness. You remember them no more; You refuse to hold me responsible for what You have forgiven. If You forgive me so completely, can I do any less?

SIMPLE TRUTH

God will never abandon a repentant heart.

Day 10

HIGH PRIEST

*For we do not have a high priest who
is unable to sympathize with our weaknesses,
but we have one who has been tempted in every way,
just as we are—yet was without sin.*

HEBREWS 4:15

FROM THE FATHER'S HEART

My child, are you struggling with temptation? Rest in Me.
Your weakness is My opportunity to make you strong. You
are not fighting your battles alone. I walked in your shoes
before you ever took a step. As your high priest, I paid the
supreme sacrifice with My own life—to make a way of escape
for you. Ask Me, and I will keep evil far from you.

A GRATEFUL RESPONSE

In the desert, garden, cities, or on the mountaintop, Lord,
You faced the temptations of Your enemies without failing.
You've experienced my sorrows, shared my joys, understood
my weaknesses, and felt my struggles. You have made me a
victor of God's dreams, not a victim of Satan's schemes.
Thank You, Lord.

SIMPLE TRUTH

*When temptation comes knocking at your door, reply
firmly, "No room."*

MASTER

"Master, Master"....
"Who is this? He commands even
the winds and the water,
and they obey him."

LUKE 8:24–25

FROM THE FATHER'S HEART
My child, you will never be at peace until you submit to My
authority. My commands are not burdensome, and neither
are they unreasonable. Have you not learned that with one
word I can send demons fleeing and dispense angel beings
to carry out My wishes? Relinquish your misplaced control,
no matter what your circumstances. You are not the captain
of your fate. I am.

A GRATEFUL RESPONSE
Lord, I hear Your quiet whispers as You comfort my heart
and calm my fears. With a simple "Peace, be still!" a thousand raging thoughts obey Your voice. Gently, You set my
sails toward land. I praise You, master of my life.

SIMPLE TRUTH
When God is in control, He puts our fears on hold.

KEEPING WATCH

*The LORD will watch over your coming
and going both now and forevermore.*

PSALM 121:8

FROM THE FATHER'S HEART

My child, do not be afraid, even when you are alone. You are never out of My sight. You can never be lost from My presence. At all times you are under My watchful eye. Listen closely, and I will tell you which direction to take. Read My words. Like a flashlight in the dark, they will light the way for you—one step at a time.

A GRATEFUL RESPONSE

At times, my eyes are blind to the dangers ahead. Emotionally and physically exhausted, I look to You, my source, to guard me. Like an ancient sentinel on guard for the enemy, You alert me from Your watchtower. Your angels are before me, behind me, and beside me.

SIMPLE TRUTH

The journey is not so hard when your eyes are on the Lord.

BREAD OF LIFE

"I am the bread of life.
He who comes to me will never go hungry,
and he who believes in me will never be thirsty."

JOHN 6:35

FROM THE FATHER'S HEART

My child, I sense your hunger to grow. No one who seeks My presence leaves empty. I will feed you, body, soul, and spirit. Come, sit at My feet daily, and we will share together. I've baked an abundance of delicious bread you've never even tasted. My manna is not of this world, but once you eat it, you will never be hungry again. I will fill you up with Myself.

A GRATEFUL RESPONSE

From the day I was born, You have known me. These hands You have designed to reach out in love; these feet You have prepared to run swiftly; this mouth You have formed to feed others, as You have fed me daily. You fill my hungry life, Lord, with Your very presence.

SIMPLE TRUTH

Why eat crumbs from the beggar's table, when we can feast with the King?

LIFTER OF MY HEAD

But thou, O LORD,
art a shield for me;
my glory, and the lifter up of mine head.

PSALM 3:3 KJV

FROM THE FATHER'S HEART

My child, when your shoulders are drooping, and your heart is heavy, look to Me. Life is filled with ordinary days, but I can make them extraordinary if you let Me. I care about your concerns. I will not only lift your eyes toward heaven, so you can get a glimpse of My glory, but I will also lift the burdens of your heart. Trust Me.

A GRATEFUL RESPONSE

Morning by morning, Lord, You lift me high above the cares of my world, far beyond the enemies of fear, depression, rejection, and discouragement. With pride and satisfaction, I can see on a clear day forever—a sneak preview of my permanent heavenly place with You. Thank You, Lord, for visions of hope.

SIMPLE TRUTH

Looking up always gives us a fresh perspective.

OUR PEACE

For he himself is our peace,
who has made the two one and has destroyed the barrier,
the dividing wall of hostility.

EPHESIANS 2:14

FROM THE FATHER'S HEART

My child, I am not your enemy. Celebrate the victory that I won for you. The prisoners of war in your heart have been set free! You are not bound by old patterns and habits anymore. I am not only your peace. but I am your bridge over troubled waters. Because you have peace with Me, you have direct access to My kingdom.

A GRATEFUL RESPONSE

Jesus, You stand as a bridge, bringing me to the Father. Your sacrifice ripped away the wall of separation and ushered me into God's presence. Your death made possible my life. The price You paid sealed my peace treaty with God. We are no longer enemies but friends, Lord.

SIMPLE TRUTH

Peace is not a feeling; it is a person.

ABBA

For you did not receive a spirit that
makes you a slave again to fear,
but you received the Spirit of sonship.
And by him we cry, "Abba, Father."

ROMANS 8:15

FROM THE FATHER'S HEART

My child, how I love to call you that! Do you know what a treasure you are to Me? Do you know how many times a day I am thinking of you? And do you know how it grieves My heart when you forget how much I love you? Did you know that if you had been the only one, I still would have died for you?

A GRATEFUL RESPONSE

You have no favorites, Lord. Your home is never too full. Your table is never too small. Your arms are never too short to embrace me—and all who call You "Daddy." I speak Your name, and a heartful of emotions well up in gratitude to You.

SIMPLE TRUTH

The Father's arms are always open to His children.

ROCK

From the ends of the earth I call to you,
I call as my heart grows faint;
lead me to the rock
that is higher than I.

PSALM 61:2

FROM THE FATHER'S HEART

My child, I hear your cries for help. I am never too busy to come. I am only a prayer away. Are you being chased by shadows of your past? Are your circumstances robbing you of strength? Come to Me. I am your rock-solid shelter. There you can rest, until your heart is strong enough to travel again.

A GRATEFUL RESPONSE

You are the stabilizing force in my life, Lord. I am but a pebble, but You are my rock, my hiding place in a world that is shaky and uncertain. Blessed be the rock. Your strength is awesome.

SIMPLE TRUTH

Jesus is the solid rock of our foundation.

PATIENCE

Now the God of patience and consolation grant you
to be likeminded one toward another according to Christ Jesus.

ROMANS 15:5 KJV

FROM THE FATHER'S HEART

My child, I understand your humanness. I never excuse sin, but I am here, ready to forgive. I see the intent of your heart. When discouragement pushes you to surrender, remember to be patient with yourself. You are a work in progress, and I am not finished with you yet. And I love working with weak vessels.

A GRATEFUL RESPONSE

How many times You give me second chances, Lord! How often You extend Your hand, welcoming me back to Your heart. You know I am dust, yet You patiently work with me, giving me time to change and developing my character into one that mirrors Your likeness. Thank You for not giving up on me.

SIMPLE TRUTH

Patience lets God write the calendar of our lives.

GATE

*"I am the gate; whoever enters through me will be saved.
He will come in and go out, and find pasture."*

JOHN 10:9

FROM THE FATHER'S HEART

My child, remember that a gate provides both protection and freedom. It will give you helpful boundaries and keep the enemy at bay. But it will also grant you entrance to sweet, refreshing pastures. I have given you the key. I am that gate. Come, and find rest for your soul.

A GRATEFUL RESPONSE

You laid down Your very life for me, Lord, as a gateway to heaven. In You I find rest, hope, comfort, and joy. Why should I look for greener pastures? Everything I desire is found in You. I love You, Lord.

SIMPLE TRUTH

*God's limits on our freedom are only opportunities to
trust Him more.*

HOLY SPIRIT

"But the. . .Holy Spirit,
whom the Father will send in my name,
will teach you all things and will remind you of
everything I have said to you."

JOHN 14:26

FROM THE FATHER'S HEART

My child, I am just as real as the air you breathe or the food you eat. When you're feeling alone or unsure of what you should do, My Spirit is there with you—a constant companion and wise counselor. Just like the disciples, you wish for My physical presence, but remember, if I had never died and risen again to heaven, My Spirit could never live in you now. This way, My presence is with you always.

A GRATEFUL RESPONSE

Like gentle breezes blowing softly, You caress each corner of my life with Your Spirit. I cannot touch You, but I feel Your warm embrace. I cannot see You, yet I know Your presence is near. I cannot hear You, but the evidence of Your love explodes my senses. You are everywhere.

SIMPLE TRUTH

God's Spirit is not for show and tell but for go and tell.

EXCELLENCE

O LORD our Lord,
how excellent is thy name
in all the earth!

PSALM 8:1 KJV

FROM THE FATHER'S HEART

My child, My world is no mistake. I designed every part of creation for your celebration and enjoyment. With every breath and every stroke of My hand, I've painted you a picture of excellence. I've given you My very best. Why? So you would recognize who I am wherever you go.

A GRATEFUL RESPONSE

Who can describe Your beauty, Lord? Who can praise You adequately? Your work in the heavens and here on earth is without comparison. Each minute detail is created perfectly with divine order. All of creation cries out in unison, "You're the best, Lord."

SIMPLE TRUTH

God is not capable of anything less than the best.

PROTECTION

"Because he loves me," says the LORD, "I will rescue him;
I will protect him, for he acknowledges my name."

PSALM 91:14

FROM THE FATHER'S HEART

My child, when your heart is full of fear, run to Me. Don't look anxiously about you, or live by "what ifs." No matter where you are, or what you're doing, just speak the name of Jesus. I will not always remove you from danger, but I am always right beside you, dispensing My angels wherever you go. Those whom I love, I also protect.

A GRATEFUL RESPONSE

Winter's blast has come at last, but in the chill of each new morning, Your warmth hovers near, Lord, to protect Your creation, both great and small. Whatever the danger, wherever we go, You are a wall of protection, guarding every step we take. In You I am safe, Lord.

SIMPLE TRUTH

The only safe place is in Jesus.

Day 23

JEHOVAH-JIREH

And Abraham called the name
of that place Jehovah-jireh.

GENESIS 22:14 KJV

FROM THE FATHER'S HEART

My child, do you worry about what you will wear, or what
you will eat? Does the future loom as a threat and not a joy?
Do you think a loving Father ignores the cries of His children? If I gave My only Son for you, the best possible provision of My love, do you not know that I will provide your
every need? Just ask. . .and you shall receive.

A GRATEFUL RESPONSE

Lord, You bless our hands, the fruit of our vines, and fill our
tables with heaven's provision. No need escapes Your wary
eye. No want goes unmet. From morning until evening, You
chase us with Your blessings, Lord. My Jehovah-jireh, how
wisely You provide.

SIMPLE TRUTH

God does not promise to supply every want, only our
needs. But He loves to surprise His children, too.

GREATNESS

Great is the LORD and most worthy of praise;
his greatness no one can fathom.

PSALM 145:3

FROM THE FATHER'S HEART

My child, there is nothing insignificant in your life. I care about it all. You may feel small in My presence because I am a God who moves beyond the finite mind. But you are important to Me. Your worship is sweet music to My ears that makes our relationship close.

A GRATEFUL RESPONSE

Down through the ages men and women have tried to understand Your greatness. Each generation searches for words to describe You, Lord. And even when I open my mouth to voice Your praise, I am speechless. I stand in awe with all of creation and applaud You, God. How great You are!

SIMPLE TRUTH

When we are right with God, we are at home in His presence.

POTTER

We are the clay, you are the potter;
we are all the work of your hand.

ISAIAH 64:8

FROM THE FATHER'S HEART

My child, did you know I designed the shape of your life? The clay doesn't ask the potter, "Why did you make me this way?" You may think your flaws and mistakes disqualify you for usefulness, but I control the potter's wheel. I have chosen you for My glory. Remember, broken vessels often reflect My beauty and light the most.

A GRATEFUL RESPONSE

With firm but gentle hands You take this lump of clay—my life—and form it into a vessel of beauty and honor. When I refuse to lie still in Your skilled hands, You patiently remake me from the marred, broken pieces. Thank You for creating me in Your image, Lord.

SIMPLE TRUTH

If we are not content with who we are, then we are
not content with who God is.

I AM

God said to Moses, "I AM WHO I AM.
This is what you are to say to the Israelites:
'I AM has sent me to you.'"

EXODUS 3:14

FROM THE FATHER'S HEART

My child, who am I? Where did I come from? Are you frustrated trying to explain My character and existence? Before the world existed, I was. Before you ever knew Me, I am. And long after this world has passed away, I will still be. I am more than a higher power or an explosion in the universe. I am beyond your understanding; yet because of our relationship, I can fellowship with you. I am that I am.

A GRATEFUL RESPONSE

"Prove there is a God," some say. But Lord, the evidence waits to be tested and experienced. I see You in a thousand sunsets, and I commune with You daily in the garden of my heart. By faith, You are and You were. You always will be the great "I Am."

SIMPLE TRUTH

He is the "I Am." And I am His.

MERCY

But because of his great love for us, God,
who is rich in mercy, made us alive with Christ
even when we were dead in transgressions.

EPHESIANS 2:4–5

FROM THE FATHER'S HEART

My child, I know your lifeless condition apart from Me. I've seen you at your worst. Yet My heart yearns for your fellowship. That's why I showed My mercy even when you didn't deserve it. I pardoned your eternal prison sentence when you lived on death row. I love you infinitely more than you are capable of loving Me.

A GRATEFUL RESPONSE

Like the woman at the well or the beggar by the road, I am overwhelmed by Your mercy and goodness. For giving Your love freely, for pardoning completely my selfish nature, for accepting me unconditionally long before I knew You—I thank You, Lord.

SIMPLE TRUTH

We sometimes settle for drops of mercy when God
wants to give us showers of blessing.

THE MIGHTY ONE

*"For the Mighty One has done great things for me—
holy is his name."*

LUKE 1:49

FROM THE FATHER'S HEART

My child, My miracles are not limited to the "spiritually elite." Does your life feel ordinary? I delight in the ordinary. Do your challenges seem impossible? I love the word impossible. Do you feel weak? I delight in making weak things strong. I am the Mighty One who has come not to save the day but to save and live through your life.

A GRATEFUL RESPONSE

The highest, most majestic mountain is but a shadow of Your strength. The vast armies of the world with their sophisticated weaponry could not match Your might and power, Lord. I am amazed that a powerful God like You would care about doing great things for me. I worship You, Lord.

SIMPLE TRUTH

With God on your side, you're always a winner.

KING OF THE JEWS

Above his head they placed the written charge against him:
THIS IS JESUS, THE KING OF THE JEWS.

MATTHEW 27:37

FROM THE FATHER'S HEART

My child, I've seen your tears as you read of My death. Never forget that I died for all people everywhere. My own rejected Me because they did not understand who I was. When they ask, I will forgive them, just as I have forgiven you. Remember always, you are royalty. You are a child of the King.

A GRATEFUL RESPONSE

It was not just Your own people, Lord, who nailed You to that cross. I, too, failed to acknowledge You as King. You, God's own Son, the best of royalty, surrendered Your life for me so I could inherit Your throne's privileges. Today, You rule as King of my heart. I bow to You, Lord.

SIMPLE TRUTH

Children of the King don't need a key to their Father's throne room.

AWESOMENESS

*For who in the skies above
can compare with the LORD?
he is more awesome than all who surround him.*

PSALM 89:6–7

FROM THE FATHER'S HEART

My child, are you struggling with the rigors of life's existence? Turn to Me. Is there a problem you don't understand? Let Me help. Look around My world. Would someone who created the mysteries of the universe abandon you without a clue? Your welfare is My business!

A GRATEFUL RESPONSE

Scientists and archaeologists marvel at heaven and earth's mysteries. All the genius of human inventions cannot compare to the creativity of Your hands. The birth of an infant, the design of the snowflake, and the intricacy of the human body are all too marvelous to comprehend. O God, You are awesome.

SIMPLE TRUTH

The beauty of a golden sunset is God's "Amen" to a perfect day.

JEHOVAH RAPHA

Praise the LORD, O my soul,
and forget not all his benefits—
who. . .heals all your diseases.

PSALM 103:2–3

FROM THE FATHER'S HEART

My child, sometimes you hide from Me in your greatest pain, thinking I will not know—or care. Other times you think I have abandoned you at your point of need if I do not answer immediately. Trust Me with every symptom—physical, emotional, and spiritual. I am Jehovah Rapha, and in My time, in My way, I still bring healing.

A GRATEFUL RESPONSE

Lord, You pour Your salve of cleansing, healing, and forgiveness over my spirit. Time and time again, I lay my complaints at Your feet, yet You never turn me away. Like the woman who touched the hem of Your garment, I feel Your power and life flowing through me once again.

SIMPLE TRUTH

God's silence is never to tease us but often to test our
abandonment to His perfect will.

LIGHT OF THE WORLD

"I am the light of the world.
Whoever follows me will never walk in darkness,
but will have the light of life."

JOHN 8:12

FROM THE FATHER'S HEART

My child, have you ever stumbled through the dark in the middle of the night? Why would you choose to go through life the same way? I will be your flashlight, giving you only as much light as you need for the moment. Stop living in the dark. Turn on the light.

A GRATEFUL RESPONSE

Wherever I go, You are a light by day and a beacon by night, shining brightly to point me to shore. There is no place too dark for Your light to shine and no corner too remote. Like sunshine on a cloudy day, You burst forth with radiance. You are my sunshine, Lord.

SIMPLE TRUTH

Just like a hallowed, shining star, His light bids us
follow Him, wherever we are.

Day 33

EMPATHY

The LORD is close to the brokenhearted
and saves those who
are crushed in spirit.

PSALM 34:18

FROM THE FATHER'S HEART

My child, do you know that when you hurt, I hurt? Pain is
no stranger to Me. I have been there, and I understand. I'll
walk with you through your fires, and I'll wipe away your
tears. When you cannot walk alone, I will carry you. Lean
on Me today.

A GRATEFUL RESPONSE

It is You, Lord, who heals my broken heart. You stand nearby,
ready to wrap loving arms around me when the hurt becomes too great to bear. When my dreams are crushed, You,
not time, are the great healer. You feel my hurts, Lord—
even more than I do.

SIMPLE TRUTH

There are no sorrows greater than our God can heal;
there are no hurts deeper than He can feel.

HOLY ONE

*"Shout aloud and sing for joy, people of Zion,
for great is the Holy One of Israel among you."*

ISAIAH 12:6

FROM THE FATHER'S HEART

My child, My nature will not allow Me to look at sin. That's why I turned My back on My own Son as He died on the cross. But because His death made a way, you can now enter the holiest of places—My presence. When I look at you, I no longer see your sinfulness. You are My child now. When I look at you, I see Jesus.

A GRATEFUL RESPONSE

How can we stand before You, Lord? Clean and pure and holy are You. Yet, in Your holiness You have made us acceptable. You have exchanged our ragged clothes of sin for robes of goodness and righteousness. With shoes removed, and head bowed, I praise You, Lord, for You are holy.

SIMPLE TRUTH

Once we enter God's holy presence, we are changed forever.

Day 35

GLORIOUS CROWN

In that day the LORD Almighty will be a glorious crown,
a beautiful wreath for the remnant of his people.

ISAIAH 28:5

FROM THE FATHER'S HEART

My child, I know you are weary at times. Like a runner who hits an invisible wall, you will be faced with choices. Will you continue or surrender? Just remember I'm on either side of you, cheering you on to victory. I will be your strength. The finish line is in sight. Run the race with persistence!

A GRATEFUL RESPONSE

When earth's joys fade, and its pleasures lose their allure, only one thing remains of value—You, Lord, and only You. A relationship with You is better than ten thousand rewards on earth. You are my crown, Lord. You are my wreath of victory at the end of the race.

SIMPLE TRUTH

The joys we experience in our journey on earth can't
compare to the treasures waiting in heaven.

DEPENDENCY

*"I tell you the truth, the Son can do nothing by himself;
he can do only what he sees his Father doing,
because whatever the Father does the Son also does."*

JOHN 5:19

FROM THE FATHER'S HEART

My child, your independent spirit sometimes gets in the way of My work. Trust Me to work through you. Dependency on Me is not a weakness but, rather, shows your willingness to obey and exchange your agenda for Mine. I did not say, "God helps those who help themselves." Rather, "God helps those who depend on Him."

A GRATEFUL RESPONSE

If You depended solely on Your Father for strength, Lord Jesus, how much more do I need You? When I try on my own, every effort fails. When I depend on my own strength, I am too weak. I desire to mirror You, Jesus. Thank You for modeling the Father. I depend on You.

SIMPLE TRUTH

Every believer needs to celebrate Declaration of Dependence Day, daily.

JESUS OF NAZARETH

"We have found the one Moses wrote about...
Jesus of Nazareth"...
"Can anything good come from there?"

JOHN 1:45–46

FROM THE FATHER'S HEART

My child, do those who know you best question you the most? I, too, found it difficult in My own hometown. Let your character be above reproach, but remember, too, that those closest to you see your humanness every day. Others see the outside, but I view the heart. Others observe your mistakes, but I see your potential.

A GRATEFUL RESPONSE

Some called You an ordinary man, the son of a carpenter. But You fulfilled every prophecy and surpassed every expectation. I, too, have found You—Jesus of Nazareth—and nothing but good have You given me. Thank You for showing me that ordinary becomes extraordinary with Your touch, Lord.

SIMPLE TRUTH

It's what God thinks of you that matters most.

Day 38

EVERLASTING FATHER

And he will be called. . .
Everlasting Father.

ISAIAH 9:6

FROM THE FATHER'S HEART
My child, someday death will sever the ties with your earthly father. Remember that I am your Everlasting Father. My arms of comfort never tire; My plans for you are always good; My relationship with you will always be secure. You can run to My arms anytime, day or night, and I will be available. You will always have a home in My heart.

A GRATEFUL RESPONSE
No matter how good or how painful our relationships here on earth, You are the One who never changes. You are the One who lovingly prepares a home for all His children. You are the One who plans our future with wisdom. For always, Lord, You are my Everlasting Father.

SIMPLE TRUTH
Children run to their Father's arms, not to win a race, but to embrace the object of their love.

HUMILITY

And being found in appearance as a man,
he humbled himself and became obedient to death—
even death on a cross!

PHILIPPIANS 2:8

FROM THE FATHER'S HEART

My child, do you long for greater service or more apprecia-tion? Remember that joy comes from My applause. Those who serve Me humbly and patiently will receive their due reward. When you humble yourself before Me, I will lift you up and set you in places you never dreamed were possi-ble. I gave My all for you with no regrets. And one day, you will hear My "Well done" in person.

A GRATEFUL RESPONSE

Heaven was at Your disposal, Lord, yet You humbled Your-self and came to earth. You exchanged a crown of glory for a wreath of thorns. You traded a royal robe for my own filthy rags. You gave up kingship for Sonship. You gave up life for death. I owe everything to You, Lord.

SIMPLE TRUTH

The applause of God is all that matters.

MY SONG

The LORD is my strength and my song;
he has become my salvation.

PSALM 118:14

FROM THE FATHER'S HEART

My child, relax and close your eyes. Do you not hear it? Not in the thunderous storm, though it is there. Not in the tornado's whirlwind, though it hovers in the air. Not in the devastating fire, though My presence follows you even there. Listen to that still, small voice. My song will rise from the ashes of your heart; in the calmness of your spirit you can hear Me. The music is My gift to you.

A GRATEFUL RESPONSE

When the music of my life has faded away, You are still there. The notes of discord threaten my joy, yet, in the distance, I hear the stirring of a new melody. Because of You, my heart can rejoice with praises again. You are the music. You are the melody. You are my song.

SIMPLE TRUTH

His song is with us through the night; when morning comes, there is light.

ELOHIM

*For the LORD your God is God of gods and Lord of lords,
the great God, mighty and awesome.*

DEUTERONOMY 10:17

FROM THE FATHER'S HEART

My child, I am not a creation of wood or stone. I am not a distant relative who never sees or knows what you do. I am holy, yet I am approachable. I am powerful, yet I am available. I am Spirit, yet I am always with you. Your praises to Me fill heaven with indescribable music and show Me that you enjoy My presence, too.

A GRATEFUL RESPONSE

No other power comes close to Yours, Lord. No other god can stand beside You. And You are not only powerful, but You are personal. You are Elohim, the Lord my God. You created me for Your glory. I bow before You as the only true and living God. Lord, I worship You.

SIMPLE TRUTH

Worship is the heart's cry for God.

SHADE

The LORD is your shade at your right hand;
the sun will not harm you by day,
nor the moon by night.

PSALM 121:5–6

FROM THE FATHER'S HEART

My child, can you feel the heat? An irate employer, heavy family demands, physical limitations that threaten to dry up your stamina? From morning until night, you can rest under the shade of My love. You will find your joy restored as you take time to remember all I have done for you—and all I will do in the future.

A GRATEFUL RESPONSE

The sun's rays cannot harden my heart or parch my joy as long as You are beside me, Lord. Even in the nighttime, Your hand is a shade from the cold and a light in my darkness. Your presence reminds me daily that I can rest quietly and confidently in You. Thank You, Lord.

SIMPLE TRUTH

Sometimes what we need most is simply to rest.

Day 43

SOLITUDE

Very early in the morning, while it was still dark,
Jesus got up, left the house and went off to a solitary place,
where he prayed.

MARK 1:35

FROM THE FATHER'S HEART

My child, a thousand things fill your mind and heart. You are so busy, but you are not invincible. Take time to meet Me early in the day. I will always meet you where you are and bring you to where I am. But you must give Me first place. Come often. I will be waiting for you.

A GRATEFUL RESPONSE

Even You needed solitude, Lord. When the crowds pressed in, and the energies seeped out, You recharged with power from heaven. I, too, Lord, need time with You to recharge my spiritual battery—so I can keep going and going and going. Thank You for Your example, Lord.

SIMPLE TRUTH

When you practice the presence of God and pursue His person daily, the performance always follows.

REFINER

These [trials] have come so that your faith—
of greater worth than gold,
which perishes even though refined by fire—
may be proved genuine and may result in praise.

1 PETER 1:7

FROM THE FATHER'S HEART

My child, if I never allowed your faith to be tested, and if I never turned up the heat, how would you experience My deliverance? Would you settle for a dull finish, or would you rather reflect My light? Hold My hand tightly. We'll walk through the fire together.

A GRATEFUL RESPONSE

Who wants to go through the fire, Lord? Yet, even in the hottest flames, You are with me. Sometimes it hurts when the outside layers are burned away. And just when I think I can stand it no longer, I see gold, Lord. I praise You for what I am becoming in Jesus. Thank You for being my refiner.

SIMPLE TRUTH

Whatever comes my way has already passed God's inspection.

LOVE

For God so loved the world that
he gave his one and only Son,
that whoever believes in him
shall not perish but have eternal life.

JOHN 3:16

FROM THE FATHER'S HEART

My child, have you walked with Me this long, and yet you still wonder at times about My love for you? What can I do to prove your worth to Me? What more can I do than to offer My own Son in exchange for your life? That was My ultimate gift to you. Because your performance could never measure up to My standards, I gave you Jesus. I love you—simply because you are My child.

A GRATEFUL RESPONSE

Lord, Your love is beyond description: unending, unbending, unconditional, and unselfish. You proved Your love for me at Bethlehem and again at Calvary. A hundred times a day, You have loved me more than I deserve and more than I can repay. I love You, Lord, more than I can say.

SIMPLE TRUTH

Love is when God writes His name on our hearts.

CORNERSTONE

*"See, I lay a stone in Zion,
a chosen and precious cornerstone."*

1 PETER 2:6

FROM THE FATHER'S HEART

My child, the most basic element of a home is its cornerstone or foundation. Without a sturdy "stone" in place, a house will shift and fall at the first storm. You, too, need that firm foundation in your life. Never forget that without Me, you are nothing. When you build upon that cornerstone, nothing can destroy that home.

A GRATEFUL RESPONSE

You are the cornerstone around which my life is built. You, a holy and righteous God, have chosen me to become a living stone—a piece of the rock. Together with other stones, Lord, You have given me the privilege of building a living temple to honor You. Jesus, You are precious.

SIMPLE TRUTH

Our hope is built on nothing less than a foundation of God's faithfulness.

ANCIENT OF DAYS

*"As I looked, thrones were set in place,
and the Ancient of Days took his seat."*

DANIEL 7:9

FROM THE FATHER'S HEART

My child, don't be troubled by the events you see unfolding in your world. I was Lord of My creation in the beginning, and I am Lord of coming events. Although you do not understand the future, or even the present, remember that I do. Live one day at a time, trusting Me, and bearing witness of Me. As Ancient of Days, I am always in control.

A GRATEFUL RESPONSE

One day all will know that the God of the future is the same God of the past. All will recognize You, Lord, as the ageless God who sees and knows everything. You have always been in the world, long before creation drew its first breath. You are the Ancient of Days, and You will rule forever. I stand in awe of Your presence.

SIMPLE TRUTH

Tomorrow is often a question on hold, but God knows exactly how life will unfold.

SPLENDOR

O Lord my God, you are very great;
you are clothed with splendor and majesty.

Psalm 104:1

From the Father's Heart

My child, I am thrilled when you reach for the hem of My garment. I have dressed you in My robe of righteousness so that you, too, can be adorned with royalty. Garments of praise become you! When you touch My heart, all of heaven rejoices with you.

A Grateful Response

Like a beautiful ornament among a thousand, twinkling lights, You shine far above Your creation. Your clothing surpasses any earthly king. There is none with which to compare Your beauty, majesty, and power. I am awed by Your brilliance and humbled by Your splendor. How great You are, Lord.

Simple Truth

With pitchers from heaven, He waters the earth and paints it with living color.

SON OF THE LIVING GOD

*"You are the Christ,
the Son of the living God."*

MATTHEW 16:16

FROM THE FATHER'S HEART

My child, when others ask you about Me, what do you say? How would you describe our relationship? Never forget who I am, and that My Father and I are one. I am God's Son, but I am also your Father. Does that confuse you? Simply rest in the knowledge that you are My child. As you stay in My presence daily, you will come to understand Me more.

A GRATEFUL RESPONSE

Lord, some say You were only a historical figure, a good man, but nothing more. You lived; You died. But You live today in my heart, the Son of a living God—not just a higher power, a spirit being, or a cosmic force in the universe. You are God's own Son.

SIMPLE TRUTH

Even when we understand less, we can love more.

RULER

The LORD reigns, let the nations tremble;
he sits enthroned between the cherubim, let the earth shake.

PSALM 99:1

FROM THE FATHER'S HEART

My child, do you know how much it hurts Me when you put others ahead of Me? Just as your own parents want to know you respect their wishes, I need your full obedience. I understand your struggle, but I will not abandon you or steer you off course. Trust Me to rule your life.

A GRATEFUL RESPONSE

Nations war against nations, fighting for the right to rule. A hundred voices cry out within me, each vying for first place in my heart. But it is You, Lord, who reigns supreme. And it is You who deserves my full devotion. Ruler of my heart, I bow before You.

SIMPLE TRUTH

Trying to rule our own life is like trying to tame a wild animal.

INTEGRITY

"Teacher,
we know you are a man of integrity."

MARK 12:14

FROM THE FATHER'S HEART

My child, My words will never pass away. Take time each day to listen to My heart's cry through Scripture. You will see that I have kept all My promises. I always will. I made them for you, and for every one of My children. You can rely on My Word—and on My integrity.

A GRATEFUL RESPONSE

Lord, how comforting to know You never lie. You speak not to tickle our ears but to prick our hearts. What others say does not sway Your words of truth. I can rely on You, Lord, in every situation to speak truthfully and to act with integrity. You are always the same.

SIMPLE TRUTH

Integrity is when you spend as much time on the backyard as you do on the front.

RESTORER

Restore us to yourself, O Lord,
that we may return;
renew our days as of old.

LAMENTATIONS 5:21

FROM THE FATHER'S HEART

My child, don't you know I am not finished with you yet? Of course there is hope for you. I have plans for you that you don't even know about yet. Your failures can be stepping-stones to success, if you will let Me restore and draw you to Myself again. I cast no one away who comes to Me in brokenness and repentance. You may never understand a love like that. Just accept it as a gift from your loving Father.

A GRATEFUL RESPONSE

Each time I step backward, You push me forward again. You take me as a master restorer would an old piece of fine furniture covered with streaks of paint and dust, retrieved from its attic burial place, and restore, polish, and renew my dull spirit. Even when I want to, You won't let me quit. I praise You for Your restoration, Lord.

SIMPLE TRUTH

There are no "has beens" in God's kingdom—only "can becomes."

WATCHFULNESS

He who watches over you will not slumber;
indeed, he who watches over Israel
will neither slumber nor sleep.

PSALM 121:3–4

FROM THE FATHER'S HEART

My child, injustice has filled the world from the time sin first entered its gates. But I have not abdicated My throne. I have not abandoned My plans. Nothing escapes My eyes. One day, all things will be made right. All scores will be settled. And although you may suffer wrongs, remember that I did, too. I am always watching for those who will be true to Me. Stay faithful, My child. I'll never leave you.

A GRATEFUL RESPONSE

Lord, our finite minds cannot understand the heartaches of the world—the violence of crime, the illness that steals a loved one, the searing pain of separation and divorce. Yet You, Lord, see it all. You, who never sleep, will one day unravel the unsolved mysteries of our lives. Thank You for watching over me.

SIMPLE TRUTH

Even in the night, He sees, He hears, and He speaks peace in the midst of our fears.

GOODNESS

I am still confident of this:
I will see the goodness of the LORD in the land of the living.

PSALM 27:13

FROM THE FATHER'S HEART

My child, do you know how much I enjoy blessing My children? Do you understand that all I want for you are good things? But it is also My goodness that forgives and prods your heart when it needs changing. It is My goodness that allows tests to come your way. It is My goodness that holds you in the palm of My hand and will not let you go. I love you, My child.

A GRATEFUL RESPONSE

I stand unworthy of any good thing. Yet You, Lord, continue to pour into my life good and perfect gifts. Daily blessings, special relationships, answered prayers, undeserved favors—You give them all, Lord. Even in difficult times, Your goodness is always evident. Thank You, Lord.

SIMPLE TRUTH

There was nothing random about Jesus' kindness. He
always went around doing good.

ROSE OF SHARON

I am a rose of Sharon.

Song of Songs 2:1

From the Father's Heart

My child, come to the garden often. I love to walk and talk with you there. In the garden I can share some of My richest and deepest secrets because your heart stills in the hush of My presence. I miss our time together when other priorities steal you away. Come, take your fill of My fragrance. And be sure to share it with others on your way.

A Grateful Response

Everywhere I look, the sweet fragrance of Your presence fills up my senses. And when I come to Your garden, Lord, just You and I alone, I can savor every velvet petal. Even the thorns pressed deeply on Your brow could not destroy the essence of Your perfume. Breathe Your fragrance through my life, Lord. You are my rose of Sharon.

Simple Truth

A garden kissed by the Son will always produce fragrant flowers.

ADVOCATE

*And if any. . .sin,
we have an advocate with the Father,
Jesus Christ the righteous.*

1 John 2:1 kjv

From the Father's Heart

My child, relax. No court in the land can separate you from My presence. No matter how deep your sin or how black your heart has been, I paid for your past. I was tried and convicted. I served your sentence. When the enemy accuses you daily, I take the proof of your innocence, the DNA—Does Not Apply—to My Father's court. My own blood covers your guilt and sets your spirit free.

A Grateful Response

Your Word silences the enemy and reminds me that You, Lord, are my advocate, my go-between, to the Father. I am guilty, yet Your very life pardoned my record. What a joy to know that my sins are forgiven, and that my future is secure in You, Lord. Thank You for pleading my case.

Simple Truth

My life cost Jesus His.

UNDERSTANDING

Great is our Lord,
and of great power:
his understanding is infinite.

PSALM 147:5 KJV

FROM THE FATHER'S HEART

My child, life is not as complex as you may think. So why do you try to figure it all out? I will teach you what you need to know. Listen to My voice. I will not lead you astray. Everything I want you to know about Me, I have told you in My Word. Read it often.

A GRATEFUL RESPONSE

My understanding is so limited, Lord. Its boundaries keep me confined and ignorant of the total picture in life. But Your ways are immeasurable. Your wisdom and knowledge surpass any standard of excellence. Like Job, I am silenced by Your greatness and infinity.

SIMPLE TRUTH

Even when traveling in waters unknown, we can
trust our wise captain to lead us home.

LAMB OF GOD

"Look, the Lamb of God,
who takes away the sin of the world!"

JOHN 1:29

FROM THE FATHER'S HEART
My child, the time for animal sacrifices is past. That was only a foreshadowing of the length to which I would go to give My love to all. I poured out My life-blood, the perfect lamb sacrifice to satisfy your debt forever. You are that precious to Me.

A GRATEFUL RESPONSE
Lord, You are the spotless, perfect sacrifice—the Lamb of great price offered on my behalf. You are without blemish, covering my own sin stains. How precious that You, God's own gentle Lamb, would silently put an end to all sacrifices. Thank You for taking my sins away.

SIMPLE TRUTH
Obedience is far better than sacrifice.

EVERLASTING GOD

The LORD is the everlasting God,
the Creator of the ends of the earth.

ISAIAH 40:28

FROM THE FATHER'S HEART

My child, when I designed you, I had eternity on My mind.
Your view of Me is limited. But one day you will share heaven's glory forever. One day the veil of your finite mind will
be lifted, and you will see the magnitude of My power. You
will understand then what eternity is.

A GRATEFUL RESPONSE

My timetable begins and ends with the present. I cannot
see the future, nor can I understand the past. But You,
Lord, are time itself. Forever and ever, You will embrace us
with Your love, Your justice, and Your mercy. You set no
limits on Your character. I praise You, my everlasting God.

SIMPLE TRUTH

In exchange for our past, He offers His throne. In
exchange for our hearts, He makes heaven our home.

SOVEREIGNTY

But you, O Sovereign LORD,
deal well with me for your name's sake;
out of the goodness of your love, deliver me.

PSALM 109:21

FROM THE FATHER'S HEART

My child, questions run through your mind faster than a sprinter leaves the starting block. It's not necessary for you to understand all the whys of your life. Because you love Me, I am working out the sovereign details of a plan so fantastic, you wouldn't believe it if I told you in advance. Give Me your trusting obedience. What you don't know now won't hurt you.

A GRATEFUL RESPONSE

Whom can I run to for help? Who understands my motives and thoughts? Who has the authority to make my enemies retreat? You are sovereign, Lord. You are the only One who has the right. You hold the key to my heart and life. I trust in You, Lord.

SIMPLE TRUTH

The Lord knows what He's doing, even when we don't.

Day 61

STABILITY

He alone is my rock and my salvation;
he is my fortress,
I will not be shaken.

PSALM 62:6

FROM THE FATHER'S HEART

My child, does your life sometimes feel like a volcano about to spew its molten contents? When you first feel the rumblings, run to the rock. Let Me hold you together in a safe place until the worst has passed. Take comfort in My stability.

A GRATEFUL RESPONSE

Lord, You are the stabilizing force of my life. When everything around me is shaking, You are that solid rock that holds me secure. At times, I may feel like falling apart, but Your stability keeps me safe. Thank You, Lord.

SIMPLE TRUTH

He is more than able—to keep you stable.

PEACEMAKER

When a man's ways are pleasing to the LORD,
he makes even his enemies live at peace with him.

PROVERBS 16:7

FROM THE FATHER'S HEART

My child, why are you disturbed by the words of those around you? Even though others at times misunderstand Me, your job is to follow Me in obedience. Be a God pleaser, not a people pleaser. Trusting Me brings sweet release.

A GRATEFUL RESPONSE

Just when I think there is no hope for peace, You remind me that You are the great peacemaker. When others discredit me, threaten my peace of mind, or push me to despair, You draw me close. I can live only to please You, Lord. Dealing with my enemies is Your job.

SIMPLE TRUTH

If we spent as much time in front of God's mirror as
we do our own, pleasing others wouldn't be an issue.

STRONGHOLD

The LORD is the stronghold of my life—
of whom shall I be afraid?

PSALM 27:1

FROM THE FATHER'S HEART

My child, have you learned when something is about to control you? If you don't close the door to the first invitation, a wrong habit will slip in and dominate your life. Let Me be your stronghold. Use My powerful name to break through every barrier. Run home to Me. I'm here to rescue you.

A GRATEFUL RESPONSE

Like deep-planted roots, unpleasant strongholds have wound themselves around my heart. Only You, Lord, have the power to remove those forts of deceit. Thank You for rooting them out and helping me to see the truth. I look to You, Lord, as my only stronghold, the One who takes my fears away.

SIMPLE TRUTH

Where weeds once grew, God helps us cultivate again,
so that "crop failure" will not rob our joy.

IMMUTABILITY

*But you remain the same,
and your years will never end.*

PSALM 102:27

FROM THE FATHER'S HEART

My child, in a world of changing values, few things remain the same. But I am one of them. What I say, goes. What I promise, stands. What I was yesterday, I still am today. I gave you My Word, just for you. You can always count on Me. My love, My faithfulness, and My goodness will always chase you in order to make you more like Me.

A GRATEFUL RESPONSE

Lord, while my emotions rise and fall like a roller coaster, You never change. You are always good, always loving, always kind, always fair. You are the same yesterday as You will be tomorrow. What a comforting thought! Thank You for Your immutability, Lord.

SIMPLE TRUTH

We are never alone in the journey of life. His presence is there—a welcome, unseen friend.

HEAD OF THE BODY

Instead, speaking the truth in love,
we will in all things grow up into him
who is the Head, that is, Christ.

EPHESIANS 4:15

FROM THE FATHER'S HEART

My child, just as a garden is made up of many varieties of flow-ers, My body—the Church on earth—includes many kinds of gifted people. Roses, carnations, snapdragons, daisies, petu-nias—all blooming together make a beautiful bouquet of praise to Me. I need your gifts. Serve Me joyfully!

A GRATEFUL RESPONSE

Whether I am an eye, an ear, a mouth, or a leg, You have cre-ated me as an important part of Your body, Lord. Only as we look to You—our Head—can the body—Your Church—function as You intend. I praise You for gifting each one of us to build up the Church. Without You, Lord, we are nothing.

SIMPLE TRUTH

Two heads may be better than one, but not when it comes to the spiritual world.

MESSIAH

"We have found the Messiah"
(that is, the Christ).
And he brought him to Jesus.

JOHN 1:41

FROM THE FATHER'S HEART

My child, some people are still waiting for My arrival the first time. They wanted a king, not a servant. They wanted relief, not true freedom. They wanted recognition, not relationship. But I am the promised Messiah, and My mission is complete. I am the One who will one day reign in My heavenly kingdom—your true home forever.

A GRATEFUL RESPONSE

Those who failed to recognize Your coming, whose eyes were blind to the truth, missed the best gift from heaven. You are the promised One, foretold for generations. You are God's own messenger, God made flesh. You are coming again. You are my Messiah—there is no one beside You.

SIMPLE TRUTH

Miracles come to those who are looking.

PURITY

Everyone who has
this hope in him purifies himself,
just as he is pure.

1 JOHN 3:3

FROM THE FATHER'S HEART

My child, I hear your cry for perfection. I know you long to feel pure—to keep your "house clean"—yet you struggle with daily failures. Rest assured, I see your desire, and I know your heart. Perfect performance does not make you pure, but the blood I shed for you. It is our relationship that matters—a Father and His child. Accept My purity. It is a gift to you.

A GRATEFUL RESPONSE

Like the finest gold, like a spotless lamb, You are pure, Lord. And though sin has blemished my heart, You have draped me in a robe of Your purity. Thank You for creating in me a clean and pure heart, Lord. I want You to shine through me.

SIMPLE TRUTH

Failure is sometimes God's way of keeping us humble.

HELPER

The LORD is with me;
he is my helper.

PSALM 118:7

FROM THE FATHER'S HEART

My child, do your tasks seem insurmountable? Are you carrying burdens far too great for you? My shoulders are strong. Lean on Me. My arms are secure. Let Me lift you up. Some days your circumstances will try to steal your strength like a thief in the night. But even in the dark, reach out to Me. I am your helper.

A GRATEFUL RESPONSE

I am only one person, Lord. Alone, I can do nothing. But with You at my side, there is no task too difficult, no dream too distant, no journey too fearful. In my past, for today, and in the future, You have been, and always will be, my helper. Thank You, Lord.

SIMPLE TRUTH

When you're tempted to despair, remember the Lord is
always there.

VINE

"I am the vine;
you are the branches."

JOHN 15:5

FROM THE FATHER'S HEART

My child, do you want to keep the branches of your life strong? Then draw from My life-giving vine. I long to produce lasting fruit in you—luscious food that nourishes not only you but those around you. Abide in Me, and let Me fill your branches with love, joy, peace, and goodness—which are all rooted in Me. Rest in Me, and I will make you a plant that reflects My beauty. I will help you grow strong through all the seasons of life.

A GRATEFUL RESPONSE

You keep me connected, Lord. I draw my nourishment from You. Only as I stay attached to You, my vine and source of life, can I bear fruit. From You flow the life-giving strength and vitality that produce sweet food for others. I would wither and die without You, Lord.

SIMPLE TRUTH

"Branching out" is permissible—as long as we stay
attached to the vine.

JOY

*"The joy of the LORD
is your strength."*

NEHEMIAH 8:10

FROM THE FATHER'S HEART

My child, the world has enough sadness. One of the reasons I have filled you with Myself is so you can spread a little joy into My world. Not just a temporary fix for the moment, but a deep down, in your heart kind of joy. You won't find it anywhere else. And My joy will lighten your load and strengthen your weary heart. Others will see it—and want the Jesus in you, too.

A GRATEFUL RESPONSE

Circumstances threaten my emotions until I realize You are the source of my joy, Lord. No matter what is happening around me or to me, You fill me up with an inner contentment that energizes me for every task. I thank You that You came so that I could have joy.

SIMPLE TRUTH

Joy is contagious. Spread some around today.

WISDOM

To the only wise God be glory forever
through Jesus Christ! Amen.

ROMANS 16:27

FROM THE FATHER'S HEART
My child, your life is so full of questions. You are like a ship being tossed on tempestuous waters. You let the salty spray paralyze you and leave you indecisive. I can see your life—the past and the future—and everything makes perfect sense to Me. I can take even your foolishness and give you a wise heart. Trust Me. Your Father always knows best.

A GRATEFUL RESPONSE
For centuries people have sought wisdom, Lord—in the pages of books, in the philosophies of men and women, in the walls of universities. But there is no wisdom apart from Yours, no knowledge but what You give. You, my wise God, know my beginning and my ending. Your wisdom holds me together, Lord.

SIMPLE TRUTH
God is working out His purpose wisely in each of us.
With some, it takes a little longer.

RISING SUN

"Because of the tender mercy of our God,
by which the rising sun will come to us
from heaven to shine on those living in darkness. . .
to guide our feet into the path of peace."

LUKE 1:78–79

FROM THE FATHER'S HEART

My child, have you seen the beauty of My mornings? Have you witnessed the birth of a new day? Glorious, isn't it? I made it for you. But that's not all. I am like that sun, rising in your heart daily to awaken your spirit and bring beauty to your life. My light will brighten every corner of your heart. I love to shine My love down on you!

A GRATEFUL RESPONSE

When the darkness creeps in, and the light seeps out, there You are again, Lord. You stand in the shadows, reaching out to comfort and renew my discouraged heart. You are the light in my dark world. You are the rising sun streaming through my window. From the rising of the sun to its descent at the end of the day, I'll praise You, God.

SIMPLE TRUTH

Like the morning sun beginning to rise is the wonder
of God's love in a child's eyes.

Day 73

SECURITY

*"I give them eternal life,
and they shall never perish;
no one can snatch them out of my hand."*

JOHN 10:28

FROM THE FATHER'S HEART

My child, when I adopted you into My family, you earned the name "child of God" forever. Nothing can separate the love I have for you—I will never abandon you. You will always find a safe place in My arms.

A GRATEFUL RESPONSE

How comforting, Lord, to know I am secure in Your hands! No wolf in sheep's clothing can ever snatch me away from You, Lord. Like a gentle shepherd, You know me by name and offer Your protection wherever I go. My name is written in Your book of life—You will never erase it. Thank You for Your security.

SIMPLE TRUTH

God never forgets a name; He loves each one of us just the same.

DWELLING PLACE

Lord,
you have been our dwelling place
throughout all generations.

PSALM 90:1

FROM THE FATHER'S HEART

My child, when I look into your eyes, I see eternity. One day My gates will open wide, and heaven, your real home, will beckon like a long-lost friend. You'll walk across and finally be home—home at last. But for now? Remember I not only want to be at home in your heart, but I also want you to be at home in Mine. Stay in My presence daily, and you will find a safe dwelling place until you reach your final destination.

A GRATEFUL RESPONSE

There are times, Lord, when I long to go home. You have created me for eternity, placing the desire for heaven in my heart. But in You, Lord, even here in this temporary house called earth, I find a place to hang my heart. You are my dwelling place, my home away from home.

SIMPLE TRUTH

We spend our energies searching for the needs of our hearts, only to realize what we were looking for was at home all along.

LORD GOD OMNIPOTENT

And I heard. . .
as the voice of mighty thunderings, saying, Alleluia:
for the Lord God omnipotent reigneth.

REVELATION 19:6 KJV

FROM THE FATHER'S HEART

My child, do you still doubt My ability? Question My authority? Wonder at My intentions? I do not wield My power without discretion. I am always firm and just. But when things go over your head, and the world appears in chaos, relax. I, the Lord God omnipotent, am still all powerful—and I am still on My throne.

A GRATEFUL RESPONSE

Like the sound of rushing waters, Your voice commands my attention, Your lordship demands my all. No power on earth can stand against You, Lord. One day I'll join the heavenly chorus with a shout of "Alleluia, to the Lord God omnipotent."

SIMPLE TRUTH

When God speaks— stop, look, and listen.

GRACE

*"My grace is sufficient for you,
for my power is made perfect in weakness."*

2 CORINTHIANS 12:9

FROM THE FATHER'S HEART

My child, when you're covered with the evidence of your convictions, and you're cowering in the shame of your condition, look up. I'm still here. Don't you know My grace is enough to cover all your weaknesses? As long as you think you're strong enough without Me, My grace is useless to you. I already know your faults. But it was My grace that made you My child in the beginning. And it will be My grace that will always lead you back home to Me.

A GRATEFUL RESPONSE

Just when I think I've had enough, when I've reached a solid wall, You appear on the scene, Lord—but not with condemnation, silence, or sarcasm. Instead, You are there holding out Your strong arms to encourage me, giving me grace to cover every weakness. Your grace is sufficient.

SIMPLE TRUTH
Duty demands; grace frees.

DEW

"I will be like the dew to Israel;
he will blossom like a lily."

HOSEA 14:5

FROM THE FATHER'S HEART

My child, is your life parched from the desert sun? Do you see no showers of blessing in sight? Don't worry. Whether it's raining outside or not, you can find a fresh start in Me daily. I am like the dew—ready to energize and refresh you for each day's journey.

A GRATEFUL RESPONSE

You are the fragrance of springtime. You are the life-giving mist on the dawn of each new day. And like a thirsty plant drinking in Your goodness and freshness, I am renewed by Your touch. Your youthfulness never changes. You are the fresh dew of my life.

SIMPLE TRUTH

Even the desert blooms in God's perfect time.

BALM IN GILEAD

Is there no balm in Gilead?
Is there no physician there?

JEREMIAH 8:22

FROM THE FATHER'S HEART

My child, why do you sometimes run and hide, licking your wounds? Did you think I would not understand, or worse, that I could not help? There is no doctor in the world who cares for you more than I do. Let My words—and My love—soothe the hurts of your heart. Whatever is troubling you, I will be your balm in Gilead.

A GRATEFUL RESPONSE

When my hurts are too deep to be spoken, and my pain seems too great to bear, You are there, Lord. Softly and tenderly, You place Your soothing ointment of love on my wounds and bandage them with Your understanding. Truly, You are my balm in Gilead.

SIMPLE TRUTH

Like a cherished quilt, God holds us close to His own heart.

GENEROSITY

*Every good and perfect gift
is from above.*

JAMES 1:17

FROM THE FATHER'S HEART

My child, I love to give good gifts to you. Do you think a
parent would deliberately present you with a poisonous
snake on your birthday? Of course not. In the same way, I
delight in giving you the desires of your heart. Some of My
gifts may not seem as good or perfect as others, but remember, miracles sometimes hide in the most ordinary places.

A GRATEFUL RESPONSE

Lord, I can celebrate birthdays, anniversaries, and holidays
all year long—all because of Your generosity. Your gifts are
perfect, always good, and always best for us. For gifts of
friendship, family, health, and salvation—but mostly for the
gift of Yourself, Lord—I give You thanks.

SIMPLE TRUTH

*Blessed are those who give generously, for they shall
reap what they sow.*

HOME

*"My Father will love him,
and we will come to him and make our home with him."*

JOHN 14:23

FROM THE FATHER'S HEART

My child, everyone needs a place to belong, a place to fit in. Sometimes you try so hard—and in all the wrong places. Don't you know that you already have a special place in My heart? Here with Me is home, a place where you will always find acceptance as My child. You have access to all the rooms. Enjoy My fellowship daily.

A GRATEFUL RESPONSE

Lord, how special it is to be part of Your family! Where else can I find a sense of belonging and a shelter for love? Where else can I find acceptance, just the way I am? You, my Father, give me a place of refuge, a place I can be myself, a place I can really call "home."

SIMPLE TRUTH

We're always at home in the Father's heart.

KING OF KINGS

On his robe and on his thigh he has this name written:
KING OF KINGS AND LORD OF LORDS.

REVELATION 19:16

FROM THE FATHER'S HEART

My child, all authority and power have been given to Me by
My Father. And one day you will share My glory and inherit all the throne privileges of My royal throne forever.
Even now, as My child, you may approach the throne, day or
night, and the King of kings will welcome your request. One
day, every knee will bow and every tongue will delight in confessing Me as you do—as King of kings and Lord of lords.

A GRATEFUL RESPONSE

Lord, no gifts or tokens of my love could ever be enough for
You, the King of kings. You never leave me standing on the
front porch of Your heart. You extend Your royal scepter, and
to my heart You say, "Come"—into Your very throne room!
Your royal decree of love can never be reversed—I am Your
child forever. I worship You as King of my heart and Lord of
my life.

SIMPLE TRUTH

> *My home is His castle, and my heart is His home; my*
> *worship belongs to the King alone.*

Day 82

MAJESTY

Out of the north he comes in golden splendor;
God comes in awesome majesty.

JOB 37:22

FROM THE FATHER'S HEART

My child, when you spend time worshiping Me and praising My majesty, it draws Me close to your heart. How I long
to reveal more of Myself to you as you wait and seek My
face. Never think you are wasting time when you reverence
My majestic name. As you praise Me, you will find My
presence real.

A GRATEFUL RESPONSE

The highest mountain peak and the most awesome wonders
of the world are only miniature reflections of Your majesty,
Lord. Yet You, a king enthroned in magnificent glory, treat
Your subjects—us, Your children—with love and gentleness.
One day, the crown You give will be my applause to You.
How majestic is Your name!

SIMPLE TRUTH

One day with God is better than a thousand in the
palaces of kings.

LIVING WATER

*"Indeed, the water I give him will become in him
a spring of water welling up to eternal life."*

JOHN 4:14

FROM THE FATHER'S HEART

My child, are you trying to live with a trickle instead of a stream? Open your mouth wide, and let Me fill you with My living water. How can you splash water on others when you are empty yourself? Sit a while, learn of Me, and drink deeply of My goodness. When you drink from My hand, you will never be thirsty again.

A GRATEFUL RESPONSE

One touch from You, Lord, and sweet fountains of joy spring up inside, a well of never-ending goodness and gratitude. With streams of living mercy, You erase my past, renew the present, and re-create the future. You are the living water, Lord, that quenches my thirsty soul.

SIMPLE TRUTH

There is a river of blessing whose never ending waters wash over us daily.

Day 84

FRIEND

*"I have called you friends,
for everything that I learned from
my Father I have made known to you."*

JOHN 15:15

FROM THE FATHER'S HEART

My child, our relationship is that of Father and child, but it is more than that. You are My friend. Friends share heart issues and never withhold the best from the ones they love. Just as My Father has revealed Himself to Me, so will I share those same secrets with you. But remember, good friends spend time together and talk—often.

A GRATEFUL RESPONSE

To think that You are not only my Father but also my friend! I treasure the quiet walks, the precious talks, and the time You spend with me, Lord. You are never too busy to listen, or to care about my needs. There's no other friend like You, Jesus. There is no other relationship on earth like Yours.

SIMPLE TRUTH

*Love is when your best friend gives up his life for you.
That's what Jesus did.*

AVAILABILITY

Yet you are near,
O LORD,
and all your commands are true.

PSALM 119:151

FROM THE FATHER'S HEART

My child, it hurts when you turn to others before you consult Me. Has My line ever been busy? Didn't I show up when your bills were due? Didn't I promise wisdom if you would just ask? Haven't I always shown My love for you? A Father loves to meet His child's needs. I'm available. Just call on My name.

A GRATEFUL RESPONSE

There is no place too far away for You to hear me. There is no distance too great for Your love to reach. Each time I call, You answer—even if Your response is "No" or "Wait a while." You are always available, always dependable, always ready to meet needs. Thank You, Lord, for Your availability.

SIMPLE TRUTH

In the emergencies of life, Jesus is always on call.

TRINITY

*"I and the Father
are one."*

JOHN 10:30

FROM THE FATHER'S HEART

My child, you wonder about My nature. How can I be three persons in one? Think about your roles. Are you a mother, daughter, and wife? A father, son, and husband? If you have seen Me, you have seen My Father. We are the same. And it is My Spirit that lives in you daily—My presence here on earth with you. Although you don't fully understand, one day you will. For now, it is enough to accept simply by faith.

A GRATEFUL RESPONSE

Your multifaceted nature is a mystery to me, Lord. You are my heavenly Father, tenderly loving and caring for me. You are Jesus, God's Son, who died that I might live. And yet You are the Holy Spirit, the One who lives inside of me. What an awesome, triune God You are.

SIMPLE TRUTH

Faith is choosing to believe with our hearts, and not with our eyes.

MORNING STAR

As to a light shining in a dark place,
until the day dawns and
the morning star rises in your hearts.

2 PETER 1:19

FROM THE FATHER'S HEART

My child, have you been stargazing lately? I long for you not to wish upon a star but to embrace the full light of who I am. I long to rise up in your heart each morning like the dawn's first light and to make you shine in this dark world. Others need your light. Rise and shine, My child! Shine your light for Me.

A GRATEFUL RESPONSE

In my darkest hours, in the midnight crises of my life, You shine brightly, Lord. There can be no darkness where You are, for You are the morning star, the most brilliant light of all. No star in the heavens, no galaxy, sun, or moon, can compare to You, Lord. You light up my life.

SIMPLE TRUTH

God holds out hope like a shining star, and leads us
out wherever we are.

RIGHTEOUSNESS

God made him who had no sin to be sin for us,
so that in him we might become the righteousness of God.

2 CORINTHIANS 5:21

FROM THE FATHER'S HEART

My child, why do you insist on keeping those worn, out-dated clothes in your closet? Why settle for a pauper's rags when I have given you the garments of royalty? You didn't earn them, and you can't buy them. I paid for them with My blood. I bought you, My child. You are in "right standing" with the Father because of My death on the cross. Wear your robe of righteousness well. It's My gift of love to you.

A GRATEFUL RESPONSE

Lord, there is no one righteous except You. No one can stand before Your goodness and purity. Yet, because of Jesus, You have made me the righteousness of God. You have given me a new set of clothes, pure and white. Thank You for Your righteousness.

SIMPLE TRUTH

When God sets His heart to love us, He never changes
His mind.

FORERUNNER

*Whither the forerunner is for us entered, even Jesus,
made an high priest for ever.*

HEBREWS 6:20 KJV

FROM THE FATHER'S HEART

My child, you need not fear the race I've given you to run.
Follow My example. I've gone before you. I've designed the
path, and I'll help you overcome any obstacles. In My power
you can accomplish anything I ask. In My strength, you can
keep your eye on the goal at all times. Trust Me for help and
direction. I'll never fail or forsake you.

A GRATEFUL RESPONSE

Lord, You have paved the path before me. You have entered
the holiest of places and have torn down the veil of sin that
separated me from the presence of God. In a sense, You ran
the race before me so that I would have a path and example
to follow. Thank You for being my forerunner.

SIMPLE TRUTH

*No matter where the path leads, God has already been
there.*

FOUNTAIN OF LIFE

For with you is the fountain of life;
in your light we see light.

PSALM 36:9

FROM THE FATHER'S HEART

My child, have you ever listened to a garden fountain? In order for you to "hear" the music of the water, the fountain must keep flowing. Come to Me often. Drink freely from the fountain of life so that you and others can always hear My music and share it freely.

A GRATEFUL RESPONSE

You sprinkle my life with showers of blessing, and my heart overflows with gratitude. I join all of creation, Lord, as I wait for You daily to bestow Your life-giving waters. You fill me up and pour me out that I might bless others, too. Thank You for being my fountain of life.

SIMPLE TRUTH

The best vessels for filling are empty ones.

JUSTICE

His works are perfect,
and all his ways are just.

DEUTERONOMY 32:4

FROM THE FATHER'S HEART

My child, what is it to you how and when I choose to bless?
I know who can handle My blessings and who cannot.
Don't fret about the ones who seem to go unpunished. You
haven't read the rest of the story. I wrote the book. I know
how it ends. And I will be just in all My dealings. Trust My
justice.

A GRATEFUL RESPONSE

Lord, it is not up to me to right every wrong or set others
straight. It is my job to love You, and to trust Your judgment. You have always been more than fair and just, giving
me much more than I ever deserved. I trust Your justice,
Lord.

SIMPLE TRUTH

When God is the judge, the rules never change.

GUIDE

For this God is our God
for ever and ever;
he will be our guide even to the end.

PSALM 48:14

FROM THE FATHER'S HEART

My child, close your eyes. Imagine you are going on a long, long journey. Be careful! There is a bend in the road. Look out! Didn't you see that hole? Watch for falling objects. You are approaching difficult and dangerous terrain. Why do you go through life at times like that—with eyes closed, oblivious to danger ahead? Don't you know I am here to guide you? I know every crevice, every pitfall, every turn. Take My hand. I'll lead you safely through.

A GRATEFUL RESPONSE

Blinded by fear, sometimes I lose my way. But You're always there to help. Even though the journey may lead me to places unknown, Lord, Your presence goes before me like a welcome, familiar friend. Thank You, Lord, for being my guide.

SIMPLE TRUTH

Following Jesus will always lead to the right path.

FOUNDATION

*For no one can lay any foundation
other than the one already laid,
which is Jesus Christ.*

1 CORINTHIANS 3:11

FROM THE FATHER'S HEART

My child, in Me you have a strong foundation. It is not built of sand. When the floods come and the winds blow, My foundation is secure. Keep trusting Me to strengthen the walls and stabilize any shifts that might threaten you. When I am your foundation, you can withstand anything.

A GRATEFUL RESPONSE

You are the foundation of my life, Lord. As long as I build upon You, my life will survive the blasts of winter cold, summer heat, autumn winds, and spring storms. You have always been my foundation that keeps me from being shaken to the core. In You I am secure.

SIMPLE TRUTH

A home is only as strong as its foundation.

SUBMISSION

"Father, if you are willing,
take this cup from me;
yet not my will, but yours be done."

LUKE 22:42

FROM THE FATHER'S HEART

My child, sometimes you act more like a rebellious teen or a reluctant child than a willing servant. If I could yield My kingly rights in obedience to My Father, can you not willingly submit your will to Me? I love to bless you! When you surrender your heart and will to Me, I can do far more with your life than you ever thought possible. Are you afraid? Will you trust your Father?

A GRATEFUL RESPONSE

Lord, it would have been so easy for You to take back Your throne without struggle, death, or submission. Yet You submitted Yourself to Your Father and gave me an example to follow. Thank You for surrendering Your life for me.

SIMPLE TRUTH

God wants more than a part—He wants all your heart.

LION OF JUDAH

*"See, the Lion of the tribe of Judah. . .
has triumphed."*

REVELATION 5:5

FROM THE FATHER'S HEART
My child, I am not king of the jungle. I am King of your
heart—and the hearts of all My children. With the lion as
My symbol, I am strength, and I am victor over anything
that would threaten My world or My children. And because
you are My child, you share in that victory and will one day
enjoy the victor's reward. But even now, you can celebrate
Me and the victory that is ours.

A GRATEFUL RESPONSE
Your name and character carry the strength of a lion, yet
You are as gentle as a lamb. One day Your strength will be
seen by all. I will join the great hallelujah chorus singing
praises to You, my Lion of Judah. You are King of all.

SIMPLE TRUTH
   *Three reasons not to worry: (1) God is in control; (2)
   God is in control; (3) God is in control.*

MY DELIVERER

I will be with him in trouble,
I will deliver him
and honor him.

PSALM 91:15

FROM THE FATHER'S HEART

My child, how precious you are to Me! I will let no one or nothing steal you away from Me. Should you stray into the enemy's camp, I have plans for a secret rescue. I am your deliverer and will fight for you. Not only will I bring you out of trouble, but I will elevate you to a place of honor—just for the sheer joy of having you back. Why? Because you are My child!

A GRATEFUL RESPONSE

You know how many times I've run to You for help, Lord. When I feel backed into a corner, lost in a maze, or imprisoned by my own thoughts, You stand ready as my deliverer. Your presence gives me comfort, just knowing I can call on You.

SIMPLE TRUTH

God cannot free unwilling prisoners.

IMPARTIALITY

Since you call on a Father who
judges each man's work impartially,
live your lives as strangers here in reverent fear.

1 Peter 1:17

From the Father's Heart

My beloved child, in your Father's house, there are no
favorites. I love all My children the same. Whatever you do
in My name will be judged by the same standards, because
I see the motive in each heart. You need not fear. I will
always be fair and just.

A Grateful Response

Lord, I'm so grateful I don't have to impress You with out-
standing performances or impressive actions. You don't cat-
egorize sin, but You look deep within the hearts of every
person and judge us all alike. Thank You for Your impar-
tiality, Lord.

Simple Truth

He who calls each flower by name loves and cares for
us the same.

Day 98

CHRIST

*"You are the Christ,
the Son of the living God."*

MATTHEW 16:16

FROM THE FATHER'S HEART
My child, who do you say that I am? Do you know that when I came to earth to be born of a virgin, I came for you? Did you know that when I died on a rugged cross, I was crucified for you? And when I rose again from the dead, I did it for you? I am the Christ, the Son of the living God.

A GRATEFUL RESPONSE
When others ask who You are, I agree with Peter's confession: "You are the Christ." You are not just a prophet who spoke the truth, a teacher of the Law, or a good man who loved everyone. You are the Son of God, and You are the Christ.

SIMPLE TRUTH
Confessing brings blessing.

FIRSTBORN

*That he might be the firstborn
among many brothers.*

ROMANS 8:29

FROM THE FATHER'S HEART

My child, My love for you is greater than you will completely understand. I loved you so much I willingly gave My life. I was the firstborn—the delight of My Father. Yet I left heaven and all My inherent firstborn rights to fulfill My Father's plan—so you could be My brothers and sisters, so that together we could share in the joys of being part of the family of God.

A GRATEFUL RESPONSE

For You to give up Your own firstborn Son—what a sacrifice for me—so that I could become part of Your family is almost beyond my powers of comprehension. Can I doubt any of Your gifts, Lord? If You gave so willingly of Your very best then, I trust Your love and judgment to give me what You feel is best always.

SIMPLE TRUTH

There's no room for jealousy in the family of God.

SON OF DAVID

"Hosanna to the Son of David!"
"Blessed is he who comes in the name of the Lord!"

MATTHEW 21:9

FROM THE FATHER'S HEART

My child, are you desirous of great events and exciting passages for your life? Remember My example. I left My Father's throne in heaven for you and identified Myself with humanity. Even though I was the "Son of David," I was but a servant to those around Me on earth. Yet My Father exalted Me in due time. My pain was your gain. My strife brought you life.

A GRATEFUL RESPONSE

Only You, Lord, would ride through a winner's circle on the back of a donkey. You had the lineage of a king, as the Son of David, and You were God's own Son. You are the King Himself. Yet You demonstrated for me the humility and submission of a lowly servant. I shout Hosanna, too, Lord.

SIMPLE TRUTH

Great endings often start with humble beginnings.

MAGNIFICENCE

All this also comes from the LORD Almighty,
wonderful in counsel and magnificent in wisdom.

ISAIAH 28:29

FROM THE FATHER'S HEART

My child, do you know how much I enjoyed planning this world for you? I designed every meticulous detail to reflect the magnificence of My Kingdom. Take time again to study the intricate makeup of the human body and My animal and plant creations. How many times does a hummingbird flap its wings to fly? How does a baby draw nourishment for nine months from its mother? How does the body so miraculously repair itself? How does a tiny seed produce such beautiful blossoms?

A GRATEFUL RESPONSE

Just like a wise farmer, You design Your plan of blessing and discipline according to the crop needed and the soil's response. I'm amazed at Your magnificence, as evidenced by Your creation of beauty, and at Your vast wisdom. Lord, You are more than I can comprehend.

SIMPLE TRUTH

His magnificence shows us our insignificance. Yet He treats us like royalty.

SPIRIT OF TRUTH

*"The Spirit of truth who goes out from the Father,
he will testify about me."*

JOHN 15:26

FROM THE FATHER'S HEART

My child, are you having difficulty discerning which voice is Mine? Quiet the noise around you. Spend time listening to My words. You don't need to wonder in doubt and uncertainty when others question you or your beliefs. The Spirit of truth, My supernatural presence in you, will lead you to the real truth about Me.

A GRATEFUL RESPONSE

Many times while You were on the earth, Lord, You prefaced Your messages with "I tell you the truth." When You left, You sent the Spirit of truth, Your own Spirit, to help us discern right from wrong and to verify Your existence. Your truth penetrates my doubting heart.

SIMPLE TRUTH

Truth is still the best policy.

THE EXPRESS IMAGE OF HIS PERSON

*Who being the brightness of his glory,
and the express image of his person. . .*

HEBREWS 1:3 KJV

FROM THE FATHER'S HEART

My child, just as your son or daughter quizzes you daily with a thousand "whys" about life, so you have unlimited questions about Me. Some answers I whisper in your spirit or relay to you through My godly messengers. But no answer will ever contradict My personal letter to you through My inspired Word. What am I like? When you see Jesus, you've seen the Father. I am the express image of His person.

A GRATEFUL RESPONSE

As a child, God, I often wondered what You were like. Did You have arms and legs like me? Did You run? Did You play? Did You sleep? Did You pray? And yet You gave me a picture, an image of Yourself, when You sent Jesus to the world. Through Jesus, I can know You.

SIMPLE TRUTH

God's children love to hear the compliment "You look like your Father."

PERSEVERANCE

*"I have brought you glory on earth by
completing the work you gave me to do."*

JOHN 17:4

FROM THE FATHER'S HEART

My child, how many times have you felt like throwing in
the towel? How many projects have you started but never
finished? How many lives have you tried to touch but felt
rejected? Are you frustrated? I was rejected, too, but I never
gave up until I finished the work My Father assigned Me.
Let Me strengthen and help you. It's never too late to start
again. Let Me work through you, and I will stamp your life
with My success.

A GRATEFUL RESPONSE

You are my example of perseverance, Lord. You started and
completed Your assigned mission. And because You suffered
through pain, rejection, and misunderstanding, with Your
help, I can make it through, also. Thank You for Your strength.

SIMPLE TRUTH

*Life's greatest lessons are learned in God's school of
perseverance.*

JESUS THE CRUCIFIED

*"You are looking for Jesus the Nazarene,
who was crucified."*

MARK 16:6

FROM THE FATHER'S HEART

My child, I know life is hard. I've seen you suffering. I've bottled all your tears. Remember that I know something about pain. I know about injustice, rejection, persecution, and death. My enemies crucified Me because they didn't understand what you know—that My death gave you life.

A GRATEFUL RESPONSE

I should have died in Your place, Lord. With every blow of the hammer, with every spike driven into Your hands, You took my sin and my inadequacies. You spilled Your blood. You gave Your life for me, Lord Jesus, the crucified, and I owe You a lifetime of gratitude.

SIMPLE TRUTH

Whatever the place or time of day, Jesus is still the only way.

FORSAKEN ONE

About the ninth hour Jesus cried out in a loud voice. . .
"My God, my God, why have you forsaken me?"

MATTHEW 27:46

FROM THE FATHER'S HEART

My child, I know you've been separated from a loved one either as a child or an adult. God could not look on the sin that I carried to the cross—your sin. To be separated from My Father—even briefly—was agony for Me. To cry out and know that He heard Me but would not respond sounds cruel. Yet that happened because of love, so you would never have to experience heaven's rejection. I love you that much, and I will never forsake you.

A GRATEFUL RESPONSE

Although I may feel abandoned or rejected by those here on earth, Lord, I have never been truly forsaken. You turned Your back on Your only Son, Your most prized possession, so that I could be adopted as Your own. You were forsaken so that I could be forgiven. Thank You for never leaving me.

SIMPLE TRUTH
We are forgiven but not forgotten.

THE RESURRECTION

*Jesus said to her,
"I am the resurrection and the life."*

JOHN 11:25

FROM THE FATHER'S HEART

My child, you've walked away from the funerals of your loved ones with fresh memories still clinging to you like grave clothes. Tears have filled your eyes as you've said good-bye to the last dreams of your heart. Remember, for those who love Me and are My children, death is but a step into eternity with Me. It is never the end but the start of forever—what you were created for! Take heart. I am the resurrection and the life. Where I am, you will be also. Find peace in Me.

A GRATEFUL RESPONSE

Lord, death could not hold You. And because of You, the resurrection, we, too, can live. Thank You that the grave is only a journey into the presence of God. You have removed the sting of death and empowered this thing called life. Now I will live in Your presence forever.

SIMPLE TRUTH

On the other side of death is the real side of life.

LOVING-KINDNESS

*I will mention
the lovingkindnesses of the LORD,
and the praises of the LORD.*

ISAIAH 63:7 KJV

FROM THE FATHER'S HEART

My child, love is who I am and what I do. I love to pour out
My loving kindness on you. A hundred times a day I am
thinking of you and of new ways that I can bless you, just
because you are My child. All My children are special to Me.
Those who love Me will see My loving-kindness daily—in
little and big ways. Celebrate that love today with Me!

A GRATEFUL RESPONSE

Each new day brings a fresh awareness of Your kindness,
Lord. The ways You care for me and Your daily faithfulness
motivate and encourage me through the difficult times. For
Your loving-kindness, Lord, my heart gives thanks for all
things, both great and small.

SIMPLE TRUTH

*Sowing seeds of kindness always reaps a crop of
heavenly blessings.*

MAKER OF
HEAVEN AND EARTH

May you be blessed by the LORD,
the Maker of heaven and earth.

PSALM 115:15

FROM THE FATHER'S HEART

My child, it's time to stop and look around again. Walk out-side. I created the world for you to enjoy. Whether you see puffy clouds or raindrops, the first buds of spring or the last falling leaves before winter, I made each season for a pur-pose. Every creature, great or small, listens for My voice. I am the Maker of heaven and earth—and that includes you.

A GRATEFUL RESPONSE

Lord, You spoke the world into existence, then flung the stars in their precise order in the heavens. You formed a spe-cial place for me to live, a home where I could reflect the glory of Your creation. I join all of nature in singing a cho-rus of praise to You, Maker of heaven and earth.

SIMPLE TRUTH

Each of God's creations is cause for celebration.

PASSOVER LAMB

For Christ,
our Passover lamb,
has been sacrificed.

1 CORINTHIANS 5:7

FROM THE FATHER'S HEART

My child, whenever I passed over the homes and saw the blood on the doorposts of My people so long ago, I did that with you in mind, as well. Whenever the priests offered a lamb as a sacrifice for sin, I was thinking of you. And when I became the Passover lamb Myself, spilling My life's blood for your sin, I did it for you—a permanent sacrifice that would erase sin forever in your heart. Enjoy My forgiveness, Child.

A GRATEFUL RESPONSE

Like the Passover lambs, whose blood was once sprinkled on the doorposts of Your people to avert the death angel's hand, Your blood sprinkled the doorposts of my heart and became the living sacrifice so I could live. What love You gave, Lord.

SIMPLE TRUTH

If God hadn't "passed over," we would have gone "down under."

HONOR

"You are worthy, our Lord and God,
to receive glory and honor and power,
for you created all things."

REVELATION 4:11

FROM THE FATHER'S HEART

My child, even when I was on earth with a physical body, I did not want others to honor Me. My entire mission was to complete My Father's work, and to bring glory to Him. Whenever you give praise to Me, you are praising My Father. Whenever you do a kind deed for someone, you are bringing honor to the Father. And when we spend time together, you are honoring My Father.

GRATEFUL RESPONSE

Lord, everything You are, and everything You do, is worthy of honor. I'm a mere servant in awe of Your creation. With all of my life, my words, my thoughts, my deeds, I choose to honor and respect You, Lord. How can I do less?

SIMPLE TRUTH

My one desire, with joy I come, is to hear my Lord
and King's "Well done."

CHOSEN ONE

"He saved others;
let him save himself if he is the Christ of God,
the Chosen One."

LUKE 23:35

FROM THE FATHER'S HEART

My child, just as I was chosen by My Father to fulfill His loving plan for the world, so I have chosen you for a special task. I know My plans for you, and they are beyond your wildest imagination. Don't worry, for each day as we fellowship together, I will unfold those plans and tell you exactly why I chose you. Trust Me.

A GRATEFUL RESPONSE

Although others questioned Your identity, You continued Your mission until death. You could have refused, but You accepted Your task with obedience. You are the Chosen One, selected by God to bear the weight of the world on Your shoulders. I'm so glad You said "Yes."

SIMPLE TRUTH

Whatever God asks, He equips you for the task.

KINSMAN-REDEEMER

"Praise be to the LORD,
who this day has not left you
without a kinsman-redeemer."

RUTH 4:14

FROM THE FATHER'S HEART

My child, even if every friend or loved one leaves you, either through death or by choice, I will always be here. You are more valuable to Me than precious rubies or fine diamonds. I bought and paid for you with My own life. I am your Father, and your kinsman-redeemer, your nearest and dearest relative. You are precious to Me. I will care for you because I have made you My own. My home is your home.

A GRATEFUL RESPONSE

You did not leave me homeless, Lord. When there was no one willing to pay the price, no one who could love and provide my needs, You stepped in and redeemed me, like Boaz did for Ruth. You are my kinsman-redeemer. The debt I owe can never match the price You paid. Thank You, Lord.

SIMPLE TRUTH

Family is a four-letter word called love.

SYMPATHY

Jesus wept.

JOHN 11:35

FROM THE FATHER'S HEART

My child, when you feel sorrow, I know what you go through. You are not alone. During those times, My arms will enfold you and hold you close until the hurt has gone. Comfort and peace are yours for the asking. And the peace I give is different from the words of others. Only I can turn your weeping into joy. Your sorrow will endure only a short time in light of eternity. In the morning, light will come, and I will restore your joy.

A GRATEFUL RESPONSE

When my heart is bowed in sorrow, so is Yours, Lord. You know what it's like to hurt. You know the feelings of sympathy, and the pangs of empathy. You've grieved at the plight of others' faithlessness. And You've mourned for the whole world, including my own sins. When I hurt, You hurt. Thank You, Lord, for the comfort of Your presence.

SIMPLE TRUTH

Tears are God's way of cleansing the heart.

GARDENER

*"I am the true vine,
and my Father is the gardener."*

JOHN 15:1

FROM THE FATHER'S HEART

My child, I long to make you like a well-watered garden
filled with the fragrance of My love and beauty—a place
where every dew-dropped petal offers praise to Me and
gives evidence that you are Mine. Let Me feed you with the
fertilizer of My Word and water you with the breath of My
Spirit. Trust Me when I cut back the dead leaves and
branches that no longer produce growth. Together, let's
walk in the garden often.

A GRATEFUL RESPONSE

You've planted a garden of dreams in my heart, Lord. You've
nurtured them carefully and pruned them painfully. But
You've given me the wisdom and skills to cultivate, so I can
tell the weeds from the flowers. Thank You for caring, master gardener.

SIMPLE TRUTH

*No matter how small the garden, each plant is a
unique treasure from God.*

COVENANT MAKER

*"I have set my rainbow in the clouds,
and it will be the sign of the covenant
between me and the earth."*

GENESIS 9:13

FROM THE FATHER'S HEART

My child, I am in the promise-making business. You need never wonder about whether I will keep My word. Just like the visual reminder, a rainbow, that I gave to let you know the world would never again be destroyed by flood, I have given you countless promises in My Word. Test them, and see if I will not pour out on you innumerable blessings when you seek to know Me intimately and trust in Me. My covenant with you is sealed in blood forever.

A GRATEFUL RESPONSE

Your rainbow was only the beginning of covenant signs between You and Your people, Lord. You are the covenant maker, the originator of all blessings and promises. Your Word has never lost its power. Each day is a rainbow, a personal promise from You, Lord.

SIMPLE TRUTH

Promises were made to be kept.

MEEKNESS

Take my yoke upon you, and learn of me;
for I am meek and lowly in heart:
and ye shall find rest unto your souls.

MATTHEW 11:29 KJV

FROM THE FATHER'S HEART

My child, your shoulders are drooping. Have you been trying to carry your own burdens again? Come to Me. My arms are strong. Let Me have your load. We are a team, remember? Relying on your own strength will only propel you into discouragement and physical exhaustion. Meekness is something I will give you, if you will rest in Me.

A GRATEFUL RESPONSE

Lord, most of my yokes are self-made, heavy burdens of my own choosing. I can learn from Your example of meekness. It is not weakness but controlled strength that can carry the world's burdens on its back, all at the same time. Thank You for Your meekness.

SIMPLE TRUTH

When the burdens of life get too heavy to bear, for the
rest of the journey, He'll carry us there.

GOVERNOR AMONG THE NATIONS

For the kingdom is the LORD'S:
and he is the governor
among the nations.

PSALM 22:28 KJV

FROM THE FATHER'S HEART

My child, when you hear the rumblings of discontent and the threats of terrorism and war, do not fear. For a little time here on earth, you will see destruction, and you may experience the vengeance of others' hatred. But take heart. I have not forsaken you. I am governor of the nations, and I still rule the world. One day earth will pass away, but you will live with Me forever.

A GRATEFUL RESPONSE

You are the governor among the nations, Lord. Your kingdom is not made with brick and mortar but with the blood of Your saints. Your mansions are not built for earthly rule but for heavenly dominion. You are fair, just, and righteous. Jesus, You reign supreme.

SIMPLE TRUTH

When you know God is in charge, you can charge ahead with confidence.

FRUIT
OF THE SPIRIT

*But the fruit of the Spirit is
love, joy, peace, patience, kindness, goodness,
faithfulness, gentleness and self-control.*

GALATIANS 5:22–23

FROM THE FATHER'S HEART

My child, do not be discouraged when you feel barren. Each
of the seeds I have planted within you I prune, feed, and tenderly nurture to its full potential. Soon you will yield the beautiful fruit of love, joy, and peace—all the qualities of My nature
that I have given you. The more you abide in Me, the more
fruit you will bear. My Spirit is the One working through you.
You can never bear fruit alone. Rest in Me today.

A GRATEFUL RESPONSE

Where else could I find a tree with perfect fruit? You, Lord,
are the fruit of the Spirit. You are the picture of perfection,
and every good fruit we need is found in You. Thank You
for planting seeds within my heart that I, too, might bear
luscious fruit for You.

SIMPLE TRUTH

Fine tuning often requires severe pruning.

CREATIVITY

God saw all that he had made,
and it was very good.

GENESIS 1:31

FROM THE FATHER'S HEART

My child, did you know that you are one of a kind? Every creation has its own original blueprints. No two birds are the same. No two flowers are ever exactly alike. I wanted you to know how very special you are to Me, and what unique gifts you have to offer to those around you. I did this so that you would reflect Me, and so that you would share in My glory.

A GRATEFUL RESPONSE

Lord, I'm amazed at Your creativity. The brilliant colors of the rainbow, the variety of creatures, the complexity of man and woman—how did You do it? One word, one voice, one command spoke the universe into being. Lord, You do good work.

SIMPLE TRUTH

The heavens declare His greatness, while our hearts
declare His praise.

LILY OF THE VALLEYS

I am a. . .
lily of the valleys.

SONG OF SONGS 2:1

FROM THE FATHER'S HEART

My child, will you just enjoy and celebrate My fragrance today? As we talk and share together, will you visualize the most beautiful and pure lily you can find, standing alone in the garden? Because that is what I want to make you. I am the lily of the valleys, and as My child, you, too, reflect My purity and beauty. You, too, will be a fragrance to others, reminding them of who I am—and whose you are.

A GRATEFUL RESPONSE

You, Lord, are a fragrant lily among the thorns in the garden. You stand alone, a symbol of loveliness and purity. Each morning I inhale Your fragrance that lingers throughout the day. You are the lily of the valleys. You are the most beautiful of all.

SIMPLE TRUTH

There is no sweeter perfume than the fragrance of
God's love.

AUTHOR AND PERFECTER OF OUR FAITH

Let us fix our eyes on Jesus,
the author and perfecter of our faith.

HEBREWS 12:2

FROM THE FATHER'S HEART

My child, don't give up. When you feel as if you've run the last lap, stop a while and catch your breath. Come rest in My arms. You will have those days when body, spirit, and emotions cry, "Enough!" When that happens, turn to Me and wait. In due time, I will give you new strength. You will not only run with energy but also mount up on wings and fly across the finish line. I initiated your race, and I will help you complete it.

A GRATEFUL RESPONSE

Lord, I feel at times like I've reached that invisible barrier halfway through the race. Every fiber of my body says, "Quit." But every whisper of faith says, "Press on." You are the author and perfecter of my faith, Lord. Thank You for running the race before me and with me.

SIMPLE TRUTH

The end of the journey is almost in sight. At the end
of the tunnel, we'll always find light.

INNOCENCE

*"I have sinned," he said,
"for I have betrayed innocent blood."*

MATTHEW 27:4

FROM THE FATHER'S HEART

My child, I paid a debt I didn't owe because I loved you so much. It was the only way. My innocence paid for your guilt—and provided for your innocence, too. Now the record is clear. Your name is secure. You have a home, not in prison, but in My heart—and in heaven.

A GRATEFUL RESPONSE

Lord, even Your enemies knew Your innocence. Without fault and without blemish, You are perfect. You paid for a crime You didn't commit and died an innocent man. Thank You for taking my guilt on Yourself. Thank You for Your example of innocence.

SIMPLE TRUTH

Just when you think you can't take any more, Jesus walks through your prison and opens the door.

FORTRESS

You, O God, are my fortress,
my loving God.

PSALM 59:17

FROM THE FATHER'S HEART

My child, remember when you used to play hide and seek? Or build forts to protect yourself from pretend enemies? When the real enemies and storms of life threaten you, and fear presses in on all sides, I will be your fortress. I am a safe hiding place where nothing can touch you. Come close. Let Me surround you with the walls of My protection.

A GRATEFUL RESPONSE

You're the wall that protects me from visible and invisible enemies, Lord. Whether it's trying circumstances or unfair criticism, You are my fortress. Like an immense castle with impenetrable walls, You seal me off from harm. I'm safe in You, Lord.

SIMPLE TRUTH

When the going gets tough, the tough hang on to Jesus.

ANOINTED ONE

*The rulers gather together against the LORD
and against his Anointed One.*

PSALM 2:2

FROM THE FATHER'S HEART

My child, the Father decided long ago how He would show
His love to all people—including you. Commissioned and
anointed by Him, I understood My mission. Heaven sang
at My birth, and hell trembled at My death and resurrection. You, too, have the anointing of My Father upon your
life. As a child of God, you have been commissioned to continue the work of grace I began. Let My power run free in
your life today!

A GRATEFUL RESPONSE

You were given, called, and set apart by God. You are the
Anointed One, Lord. God placed His blessing upon Your
head and confirmed the work of Your hands. You have the
mark of heaven on Your life. You are a promise fulfilled and
a dream come true. I worship You, Lord.

SIMPLE TRUTH

Anointing always follows His appointing.

STEADFASTNESS

For he is the living God,
and stedfast for ever.

DANIEL 6:26 KJV

FROM THE FATHER'S HEART

My child, you can trust Me as I will never fail you. Others will leave you hanging and use you for their own selfish purposes, but I am always the same. Although you may question Me at times and fail to understand My reasons, you can rest in the assurance that My character is steadfast, never changing. Just like My love for you.

A GRATEFUL RESPONSE

Lord, You never change Your mind on a whim. You're not like a ship on the sea, driven and tossed by harsh winds. Your heart, thoughts, will, and purpose are set forever. That gives me incredible security and faith. Thank You for Your steadfastness, Lord.

SIMPLE TRUTH

Faithfulness is when God says "Amen" to the end of your task.

CHIEFEST AMONG TEN THOUSAND

My beloved is. . .
the chiefest among ten thousand.

SONG OF SOLOMON 5:10 KJV

FROM THE FATHER'S HEART

My child, you are My beloved, too. Ours is a love relationship unlike any other. I love spending time with My children. I love being the chief ruler of your life, and I am jealous for your attention. Let Me help you with your priorities. Nurture this relationship we have. It is your most precious possession.

A GRATEFUL RESPONSE

Lord, Your face is a reflection of beauty. Your features are greater than any other. Though I cannot see You with human eyes, my spirit chooses You above all other loves. You are the chiefest among ten thousand, and You rule with honor and dignity. Lord, You are my hero.

SIMPLE TRUTH

How does God love thee? Unconditionally.

MEDIATOR

For there is one God and one mediator
between God and men, the man Christ Jesus,
who gave himself as a ransom for all men.

1 TIMOTHY 2:5–6

FROM THE FATHER'S HEART

My child, it is not necessary for you to rely on good deeds. Your performance could never earn enough "points" to grant My Father's pardon. Nor do I want you to live in regret over past failures, trying to walk on eggshells to please Me. I am your mediator. Because of My death, your past is forgiven, and because of My Spirit living in you, you now have the power to choose right. Your love for Me now motivates you to live for Me. When the enemy accuses you, send him to Me. Through Me you have access to heaven's throne.

A GRATEFUL RESPONSE

Like the woman accused by hypocritical Pharisees, I feel no condemnation for my confessed thoughtless actions, only forgiveness and love. You stand before the Father as my mediator, pleading my case. I need not fear my day in court because You are there, Lord.

SIMPLE TRUTH

He intercedes for you so you can proceed to Him.

SUFFICIENCY

Not that we are sufficient of ourselves
to think any thing as of ourselves;
but our sufficiency is of God.

2 CORINTHIANS 3:5 KJV

FROM THE FATHER'S HEART

My child, if you try to operate in your strength, you will fail every time. Every gift you own comes from Me. Every ability you use, I gave you. My power is available to you. I am your sufficiency. Don't worry about anything. Tell Me your needs. I know them anyway, but I love to hear you ask, just like a Father who is eager to provide for His child.

A GRATEFUL RESPONSE

Contrary to what some say, Lord, there is enough. You have given me more than I could ever ask for, more than I could ever imagine. Before I even need anything, You have already supplied it. In myself, I have nothing. But through You anything is possible. Thank You for Your sufficiency, Lord. You are more than enough.

SIMPLE TRUTH

All that He is, is all that we need.

ARCHITECT AND BUILDER

*For he was looking forward to the city with foundations,
whose architect and builder is God.*

HEBREWS 11:10

FROM THE FATHER'S HEART

My child, you won't believe the surprises I have waiting for you. Your finite mind could not grasp the beauty of the home I've designed especially for you. I've pored over every detail. Heaven is not a figment of your imagination. It is the reality of Mine. I should know. I built it with My own hands. And I want your heart to reflect the kind of beauty that heaven holds for you someday. Trust Me. I'll keep renovating your "home" often.

A GRATEFUL RESPONSE

You've prepared not just a beautiful home for me, Lord, but an entire city. Our blueprints could not compare to Your master plan. Strong foundations, elegant mansions, streets of gold aglow with Your light—You are the architect and builder of heaven. I can't wait, Lord.

SIMPLE TRUTH

Heaven is God's way of saying, "Welcome home."

MIRACLE WORKER

You are the God who performs miracles;
you display your power among the peoples.

PSALM 77:14

FROM THE FATHER'S HEART

My child, why is it so easy for you to believe My miracles so long ago but question My power today? My power hasn't changed—but hearts have. Trust Me with childlike faith. Children don't ask for signs but for felt needs and desires. Ask Me anything in the name of Jesus, according to My will. And always be willing to accept My answer, no matter what it is. Most people miss My miracles because they stop looking, or because they look in the wrong places.

A GRATEFUL RESPONSE

Lord, You have always performed miracles. From the beginning of time, You created the world out of nothing. You pushed back the seas, blinded the enemy, turned water to wine, healed the sick, and raised the dead. There is nothing impossible for You, Lord. Every day is a fresh miracle! You are the miracle worker.

SIMPLE TRUTH

God is the only one who can make something out of nothing.

DIVINITY

*His divine power
has given us everything
we need for life and godliness.*

2 PETER 1:3

FROM THE FATHER'S HEART

My child, I know it is difficult for you to think beyond the lines. But you have the mind of Christ. His divine nature is in you, speaking to you, directing you daily. There is never a reason for fear or anxiety because, as your divine Savior and God, I never let you out of My sight. I know every need before you ask, every hurt before you cry, every joy before you celebrate.

A GRATEFUL RESPONSE

Perfectly human, yet perfectly divine, You live in this world—and in my life—with all power. Your origin is heaven, yet Your destiny is the hearts of all people. How marvelous to share in Your divinity as heirs! Lord, I praise You for Your divinity.

SIMPLE TRUTH

To err is human; to fellowship with God, divine.

FATHER OF THE HEAVENLY LIGHTS

Every good and perfect gift is from above,
coming down from the Father of the heavenly lights,
who does not change like shifting shadows.

JAMES 1:17

FROM THE FATHER'S HEART

My child, I am not like a shadow that moves with the rays of the sun. Everything in My presence radiates My light, for I am the Father of the heavenly lights. The sun, moon, and stars reflect My glory. The angels who serve Me daily wear My light on their wings and glow with My presence. And so do you. Look at Me often, and I will reflect My light through you.

A GRATEFUL RESPONSE

In Your entire world there is one light that never changes. With You, Lord, there is no darkness. You are the Father of all heavenly lights. In Your presence the sun need not shine, for You are the brightness of creation. How brilliant is Your light!

SIMPLE TRUTH

The light of the world is still Jesus.

Day 134

BLESSED HOPE

While we wait for the blessed hope—
the glorious appearing of
our great God and Savior, Jesus Christ.

Titus 2:13

From the Father's Heart

My child, I know there are times when hope seems like a mirage in the desert—appearing one minute, fading the next. But remember I am your blessed hope. When you put all your expectations in Me, you will never be disappointed. As My child, your hope is not built upon earthly plans that may fail, but in eternal values that last forever. Let Me fill you with joyful hope today—enough to last for all your tomorrows.

A Grateful Response

Lord, You build a bridge of hope where there is no understanding. You then carefully escort me to where my heart can find renewal for the journey ahead. When life disappoints, when dreams diminish, and when friends disappear, You, Lord, remain my blessed hope.

Simple Truth

Hope-filled hearts come from trust-filled lives.

REMEMBRANCE

"Can a mother forget the baby at her breast. . . .
Though she may forget,
I will not forget you!"

ISAIAH 49:15

FROM THE FATHER'S HEART

My child, how could I ever forget who you are? I have engraved your name on the palm of My hand; I have sealed it in My heart and in the book of life. I created you, and I know every path you've ever taken, every decision you've ever made, every word you've ever thought or spoken. I remember the names of all My children. I will never forget any of them, for they are all special to Me.

A GRATEFUL RESPONSE

Like a mother tenderly nursing her baby, You have nurtured me, Lord. You've guided my steps, overlooked my mistakes, encouraged my efforts, and praised my achievements. You forgive and forget my sins, but You never forget me. Thank You, Lord.

SIMPLE TRUTH

Always remember: The Lord never forgets.

SCARLET CORD

*And she tied the scarlet cord
in the window.*

JOSHUA 2:21

FROM THE FATHER'S HEART

My child, you have often heard that there is power in the blood. My power. My blood. I am the scarlet cord that runs through your spirit, giving it life, power, and strength. Whenever you doubt My presence or think I do not care, remember the cord. Remember the blood I shed for you. Remember My sacrifice and rejoice in the love I have for you.

A GRATEFUL RESPONSE

Like the heavy rope resting outside Rahab's window, You are the scarlet cord that runs throughout Your Word. I can trace the paths of Your blood. I can track the tears of Your love. I can mark the record of Your faithfulness. And they all point to You, my loving God.

SIMPLE TRUTH

God's scarlet cord of love is the tie that binds His children together.

GUARANTEED DEPOSIT

*Now it is God who has made us for this very purpose
and has given us the Spirit as a deposit,
guaranteeing what is to come.*

2 CORINTHIANS 5:5

FROM THE FATHER'S HEART

My child, do you long to exchange your earthly clothes for
heavenly garments? Do you know why death, illness, and
difficult circumstances enter your life? Partly to make you
homesick and keep you focused on what is to come, not
what you see here. How do you know something better is
coming? My Spirit, your guaranteed deposit, assures you.
My Spirit bears witness that a wonderful future awaits you
beyond this world!

A GRATEFUL RESPONSE

How do I know Your promises are true? How can I believe
in someone I've never seen or touched? Because I have Your
Spirit, Lord—my guaranteed deposit, my down payment,
the One who lives inside and testifies to Your goodness.
Lord, You give wonderful dividends.

SIMPLE TRUTH

*God has no faith-back guarantee. Once you're His
child, you're His forever.*

DAILY IN YOUR PRESENCE—149

AUTHENTICITY

*"These are
the true words of God."*

REVELATION 19:9

FROM THE FATHER'S HEART

My child, few things in this life are authentic. Avoid that which is false. Don't hide the real you under a bushel of pride, discontent, or comparison. Learn from Me. I'm the real thing. You cannot see Me in person or hear My voice audibly. You cannot feel the nail prints in My hand as Thomas did. But I am more real than your dearest loved one. When you reach out in faith, I will take your hand. I am always by your side, and always in your heart.

A GRATEFUL RESPONSE

People are always searching for the real thing, the genuine article, the pearl of great price. I, too, looked in vain until I found You, Lord. You are more authentic than the purest diamond, more precious than the costliest pearl. Jesus, You are the true God.

SIMPLE TRUTH

*Where else can fellowship be so sweet—than to sit in
His presence at Jesus' feet?*

DISCIPLE MAKER

*"By this all men will know that you are my disciples,
if you love one another."*

JOHN 13:35

FROM THE FATHER'S HEART

My child, do you really desire to be My disciple? Are you willing to pay the price? Are you afraid of where I might lead you? Of what might be taken away? No one who has followed Me has ever left behind more than I will give Him in exchange. Spend time with Me daily. Listen well. I will make you My disciple. In the past you have lived for yourself. But when you let My love flow through you, others will know you are truly My disciple.

A GRATEFUL RESPONSE

From an unlikely band of misfits, Lord, You chose Your disciples. You poured Your life into theirs, teaching them, guiding them, and walking with them daily. As a disciple maker, You taught them how to love. Because of Your eternal investment I, too, can become Your disciple.

SIMPLE TRUTH

God doesn't expect your best. He wants your all.

BAPTIZER

*"He will baptize you with
the Holy Spirit
and with fire."*

MATTHEW 3:11

FROM THE FATHER'S HEART

My child, because My Spirit has baptized you with love and power, you have been filled with every good thing you need to complete the work I gave you. But that filling is ongoing. Do not quench My Spirit with disobedience. Run to Me at the moment of your betrayal, and let My purifying fires do their work through you. I will immerse you daily with My love, My grace, My goodness, and My power.

A GRATEFUL RESPONSE

Lord, You baptized me not with water, but with Your Spirit of love. You placed a holy fire in my heart, an unquenchable flame that burns with the desire to know You, and to testify to Your faithfulness daily. You are my baptizer, Lord. Thank You for keeping the fire burning.

SIMPLE TRUTH

It's hard to get a fire going when the wood is wet.

FORCEFULNESS

On reaching Jerusalem,
Jesus entered the temple area and began driving out
those who were buying and selling there.
He overturned the tables. . .and the benches.

MARK 11:15

FROM THE FATHER'S HEART

My child, remember My Father's house is a house of prayer, a holy place, a place where heaven feels free to call, and My Spirit has freedom to move. In the same way, I want your heart, My dwelling place in you, to be a place of honor. I force My way into no one's heart. You invited Me in. But when My Father's reputation is at stake, I will act in whatever way to restore holiness and maintain integrity. I will help you keep this home pure.

A GRATEFUL RESPONSE

In defense of Your Father's house and reputation, You showed us Your forcefulness, Lord. I, too, want to defend Your name. In times when courage needs to shine the most, in moments when truth demands action, Your mighty strength is always with me.

SIMPLE TRUTH

Courage is the ability to act on your own convictions,
no matter what others do.

WEEPING PROPHET

Oh, that my head were a spring of water
and my eyes a fountain of tears!
I would weep day and night for the slain of my people.

JEREMIAH 9:1

FROM THE FATHER'S HEART
My child, today mothers or fathers might reject their children, but I will never reject you. It gives Me no pleasure to see you suffer because of stubborn self-will. I weep over My children—tears of sadness when they turn away, and cries of joy when they return. I once wept for you with My life. I was bruised and crushed for your rebellion. I was like the weeping prophet. But when you—and all My children—return to Me, there will be a time of great celebration. I never cease to love you.

A GRATEFUL RESPONSE
The prophet Jeremiah was a picture of You, Lord. You were the "weeping prophet," crying over the rebellion of Your people. And even today, how Your heart must grieve over our sin. Yet, You promised restoration when we return to You. What a relief to know You won't reject us!

SIMPLE TRUTH
There's no place like God's home.

KING OF GLORY

Who is he, this King of glory?
The LORD Almighty—
he is the King of glory.

PSALM 24:10

FROM THE FATHER'S HEART

My child, the relationship we share has earned you a place in My kingdom. Open the gates of your heart wide and let Me, your King of glory, reign over every area of your life. When you give Me the key, you have full assurance that I will rule your heart wisely. And then one day I will take you to a far better home than the one you live in now. All My children will have the privilege of sharing My glory in My heavenly palace.

A GRATEFUL RESPONSE

One day I'll join the winner's circle, giving praise and honor to the One who leads the final battle. You, Lord, are my King of glory. My one desire is to come with joy, honor You, and hear my King's applause. Together with You, Lord, is a forever place to be.

SIMPLE TRUTH
Where self ends, God begins.

Day 144

RESISTANCE

Jesus answered,
"It says:
'Do not put the Lord your God to the test.'"

LUKE 4:12

FROM THE FATHER'S HEART

My child, I know you so well. Like Peter, you sometimes think you are invincible—beyond gross sinfulness. Even as My child, you are capable of anything. Never turn away from Me for a moment, or you will find yourself in enemy territory. I will not prevent you from being tempted, but I will deliver you from the temptation. Remember, I was tempted, too. I understand. And I will show you a way out. I will also be there to catch you if you fall.

A GRATEFUL RESPONSE

With the authority of Your Father's words, and the power of the Spirit, You sent Your worst enemy away. Your resistance to Satan's schemes and desire for power gives me hope and an example to follow. There's no temptation too great for me to bear, Lord. You're on my side.

SIMPLE TRUTH

If you want to avoid temptation, don't go window shopping.

FULLNESS OF THE DEITY

*For in Christ all the fullness of
the Deity lives in bodily form. . .
who is the head over every power and authority.*

COLOSSIANS 2:9–10

FROM THE FATHER'S HEART

My child, all that I am I have given to you. All that I am is because of My Father. My words carry no authority without My Father's stamp of approval. I am the fullness of the Deity, God-man, the One who gives all others their right to be leaders in high places. When you acknowledge Me as your authority, you are acknowledging God as the ultimate ruler of your life. Through Me, you, too, have the fullness of Christ.

A GRATEFUL RESPONSE

Everything God wanted to show us, He showed in You, Lord. All of God's character—His goodness, greatness, power, and authority—is in You. And You have given me Your fullness. You are the fullness of the Deity. In You I am complete.

SIMPLE TRUTH

We are known not so much by what we believe, but in whom we believe.

A JEALOUS GOD

Do not worship any other god,
for the LORD, whose name is Jealous,
is a jealous God.

EXODUS 34:14

FROM THE FATHER'S HEART

My child, do you crave unswerving devotion from your spouse? The thought of betrayal is enough to fire up every jealous nerve in your body and spirit. Of course I desire all of your attention, all of your time, and all of your self. I am a jealous God, but not because of a fear of being replaced, as you feel. I love you so much that I am not willing for anyone to steal your heart away. I gave My life for you because I want none to perish.

A GRATEFUL RESPONSE

Your jealousy is not a flaw in Your character, Lord. Because You love me so much, You demand no less than my total devotion. You tolerate no other loves. In my negligence, I often build idols of my own choosing. But how can my heart truly worship another but You, Lord? Only You satisfy.

SIMPLE TRUTH

If left alone, idols in the heart will soon turn to stone.

TENDERNESS

He gathers the lambs in his arms
and carries them close to his heart;
he gently leads those that have young.

ISAIAH 40:11

FROM THE FATHER'S HEART

My child, you are indeed one of My precious lambs. I know your nature. Like a sheep that easily wanders astray, your cries bring Me to your side in a moment. When you are hurting, I do not pour salt on your wounds. Instead, you will feel My soothing love and tender touch, healing the cuts you have sustained. When you cannot walk alone, I will carry you gently until you have safely reached green pastures again.

A GRATEFUL RESPONSE

Just like a caring shepherd, You carry me as one of Your lambs close to Your heart. I love Your tenderness, the way You nurture me and soothe my bleeding wounds. I want to stay close, Lord, listening for Your heartbeat, keeping my eyes on You. I love You, Lord.

SIMPLE TRUTH

There are no greener pastures than God's own backyard.

LORD OF THE SABBATH

Then Jesus said to them,
"The Son of Man is Lord of the Sabbath."

LUKE 6:5

FROM THE FATHER'S HEART

My child, it's useless for you to work from morning until night, seven days a week. Not only does your body need rest, but your spirit and emotions must recharge, as well. Just as I ceased my creation work after six days, you, too, must take time to celebrate life—and to enjoy My presence. Worship is vital to our relationship. When you love Me with all your heart, soul, and mind, how you spend the "Sabbath" will not be an issue.

A GRATEFUL RESPONSE

I hear so many opinions on how to spend Your day, Lord. Is it Saturday or Sunday? A day of rest or a day of worship? Is it a day for refusal or a chance for renewal? Whatever it means, I know You created that day for our benefit—and for Your glory. Jesus, You are Lord of the Sabbath.

SIMPLE TRUTH

Sleep is sweet and love complete when we rest under the covers of God's love.

BELOVED

*I am my beloved's,
and my beloved is mine.*

SONG OF SOLOMON 6:3 KJV

FROM THE FATHER'S HEART

My child, we have a wonderful love relationship that I want to guard at all costs. I am your beloved, and I feel the same way about you. In that sacred romance, I long for you to stay close to Me. There is no one else who will meet your needs like I will. There is no one who will ever love you like I do. Come, sit beside Me. I love to share My inmost secrets with you.

A GRATEFUL RESPONSE

Your love is like no other, Lord. With You, there is a belonging and a warm sense of security. I love to walk and fellowship with You in the cool of Your garden, or by the warmth of a fire. When You speak, my heart and spirit leap to join my beloved One. Wherever You are, Lord, is where I want to be.

SIMPLE TRUTH

If love were heaven's only gift, it would be enough.

POWER

*So great is your power that
your enemies cringe before you.*

PSALM 66:3

FROM THE FATHER'S HEART

My child, look around you today, and you will see evidences of My power. Come and see My awesome works. They were created for you! I'm the One who turned dry land into raging rivers; it was My power that swallowed up the enemies who threatened My people. And it is My power that will protect you. Stand firm! With Me beside you, fear flies out the window.

A GRATEFUL RESPONSE

Lord, I am like an ant when compared to You in all Your power. I fear You, but it is a reverent fear. Because of Your strength, and because You are a God of power, I am not afraid. My enemies scatter in all directions, all at the spoken name of Jesus. Thank You for being a powerful God.

SIMPLE TRUTH

In the presence of God, fear grows dim, and hope glows bright.

CHIEF COMMANDER OF HIS ARMY

The LORD thunders at the head of his army;
his forces are beyond number,
and mighty are those who obey his command.

JOEL 2:11

FROM THE FATHER'S HEART

My child, did you know I recruited you into My army because of the awesome potential I saw in you? As with Gideon, I recognized you as a "mighty one of valor." When you follow Me and pay close attention to My commands, together we can make an invincible team against the enemy. There are times I may ask you to stand still and let Me fight for you. And at other times, I will give you precise instructions as an enlisted soldier. Trust My words. I am your chief commander and will always bring victory.

A GRATEFUL RESPONSE

Lord, in every battle I've ever faced, You've been there as my chief commander. At times I've gone AWOL, cowering under the pressure of my enemy. When I followed Your leadership, sweet victory always came. In spite of my failures, You reward me with the medal of honor: Your unconditional love.

SIMPLE TRUTH

God's Word is our weapon; His Spirit is our sword.

DECISIVENESS

"Come, follow me," Jesus said,
"and I will make you fishers of men."

MATTHEW 4:19

FROM THE FATHER'S HEART

My child, long before you were born, decisiveness was a part of My nature. Every detail of creation I planned carefully, with no shadow of turning. Long ago I decided the color of your hair and eyes, your height, your personality—and which gifts would suit you perfectly. Long ago I set My heart to love you as My own, just as I did My disciples and all My children.

A GRATEFUL RESPONSE

Lord, I admire Your decisiveness. You followed through faithfully with Your plan for discipleship, choosing each man carefully. You knew the perfect timing for every divine encounter. When decisions were necessary, You moved wisely. During temptation, at Your trial, and even at Your death, You were decisive, always acting unselfishly for my benefit.

SIMPLE TRUTH

Responsibility is our ability to make the right choice.

GOD OF RETRIBUTION

For the LORD is a God of retribution;
he will repay in full.

JEREMIAH 51:56

FROM THE FATHER'S HEART

My child, never let bitterness take root in your heart. When you feel angry, come to Me, and let's talk about it. Don't take it out on someone else. Untreated, bitterness can eat at you and grow like a cancer throughout your system. Instead, empty your garbage at My feet, and let Me take care of your enemies. I am the God of retribution, not you.

A GRATEFUL RESPONSE

Although revenge may seem sweet, it will only sour my heart and stifle my life. You know how to deal with my enemies better than I, Lord. You never overlook sin or injustice, and You are always watching out for Your own. You are the God of retribution; vengeance is Yours.

SIMPLE TRUTH

Render unto God the vengeance that belongs to God.

Day 154

ANTICIPATION

*"I am going there to prepare a place for you. . . .
I will come back and take you to be with me
that you also may be where I am."*

JOHN 14:2–3

FROM THE FATHER'S HEART

My child, I'm so excited about your new forever room.
You're going to love it. As long as I keep you here on earth to
bring Me glory, we will work on the rooms of your heart
together. But in the meantime, My anticipation grows for
the time when I'll unveil your final home. It's so beautiful—
you won't believe it!

A GRATEFUL RESPONSE

Have You really prepared a place for me, Lord? Do You
have room in Your mansions for one like me? You wait there
with anticipation until the time You call me to join Your
presence. How precious that You care so much! Lord, I'm
coming home to You soon.

SIMPLE TRUTH

*God spares no expense to add on more rooms to His
house.*

BRIDEGROOM

"At midnight the cry rang out:
'Here's the bridegroom!
Come out to meet him!' "

MATTHEW 25:6

FROM THE FATHER'S HEART

My child, not even I know the time when I, your bridegroom, will return for My church and My children. Only My Father knows. Stay close to Me and keep the light on in the window of your heart. Watch with anticipation for My return. And when the time is right, My bride, you'll shout with joyful heart, "Here comes the groom!"

A GRATEFUL RESPONSE

Lord, I can only imagine the wedding day, when You, my bridegroom, say to me, "Come!" With fluttering heart, and trembling hands, I'll join my long-awaited love and celebrate an eternity of joy in the home You have prepared for me. Lord, there is no other love but You. Your bride is ready!

SIMPLE TRUTH

The bridegroom never breaks His vows. He loves you today, tomorrow, and forever.

Day 156

TEACHER

"You call me 'Teacher' and 'Lord,' and rightly so,
for that is what I am. . . . I have set you an example."

JOHN 13:13, 15

FROM THE FATHER'S HEART

My child, don't worry about what you don't know. Knowledge is what you learn from a textbook; wisdom is what comes from My Father. My Spirit will be your teacher when you enroll in My lifelong school of learning. As a diligent student, do your homework well simply because you love Me. With Me, class is never out. I will be faithful to teach you daily.

A GRATEFUL RESPONSE

Lord, all the degrees of higher learning could not teach me what You can. You are knowledge itself. You are my teacher, and from You come the wisdom and application for right and joyful living. With the heart of a servant, You set an example. Lord, I want to sit at Your feet daily.

SIMPLE TRUTH

Character was never built—or taught—in a day.

OBEDIENCE

Although he was a son,
he learned obedience from what he suffered.

HEBREWS 5:8

FROM THE FATHER'S HEART

My child, like most parents, I need your obedience. Without the boundaries My love outlines for you, you would become an easy target for every kind of harmful influence. Your obedience is your safety net, for it ushers in My guaranteed protection and blessing daily. Sometimes I allow difficult things to enter your life in order to conform you to My image. Even as I learned to submit to My Father, you must do the same, knowing it will draw you closer to the Father's heart.

A GRATEFUL RESPONSE

If You, the perfect Son of God, had to learn obedience, how much more do I need that lesson! Lord, my suffering often brings obedience, too, but it usually comes through painful rebellion first. Thank You for understanding my heart's desire: to obey You at all costs.

SIMPLE TRUTH

What failure can teach you depends on what you are
willing to learn.

VICTORIOUS ONE

*The horse is made ready for the day of battle,
but victory rests with the LORD.*

PROVERBS 21:31

FROM THE FATHER'S HEART

My child, sometimes you act as if you are still a prisoner of
war. Perhaps you are looking for strength and victory in all
the wrong places. Let Me fight your battles. The only way
you will ever experience victory is when I am on your side.
And I am on your side. When I fight for you, no one can
stand against you. I am the victorious One.

A GRATEFUL RESPONSE

Lord, nations fill their arsenals, each hoping to surpass the
other's strength in the event of war. Whether in corporate
or personal battles, in life or in death, we cannot win without You, Lord. You are the victorious One. Thank You for
fighting our battles.

SIMPLE TRUTH

*Don't sweat the battles when the King is in
command.*

JEHOVAH-SHAMMAH—
THE LORD IS THERE

"And the name of the city from that time on will be:
THE LORD IS THERE."

EZEKIEL 48:35

FROM THE FATHER'S HEART

My child, I will be your source of strength when your heart is failing. I will hold your hand when your steps falter. There will never be a time when you are truly alone, even though you may feel My presence is as distant as the stars in the heavens. I am Jehovah-shammah, the God who is always with you, always ready to help, the One who constantly celebrates the joy of having you as My child.

A GRATEFUL RESPONSE

Sometimes You lead me over rugged mountain trails and through dark valleys. Though Your face is hidden, and Your voice is silent, I sense Your protection all around me. I cannot escape Your presence, nor do I want to. You are Jehovah-shammah. You, Lord, are always there.

SIMPLE TRUTH

Wherever God leads, our hearts can follow with
confidence.

PROMPTNESS

The eyes of all look to you,
and you give them their food at the proper time.

PSALM 145:15

FROM THE FATHER'S HEART

My child, I created time. Do I not have the right to decide what is the "proper" time for all things? I have never been late. What you perceive as tardiness or indifference, I call a purposeful delay—only because I have ordained perfect timing which you know nothing about. Whenever you call, I always answer. My line is never busy. When you seek Me, you will always find Me. Promptness is something I delight in showing to My children.

A GRATEFUL RESPONSE

In my impatience, Lord, I often cry, "Hurry up!" You are never in a hurry, yet You are always on time. Though I'm sometimes tardy, You've never missed an appointment. For Your patience with my grumbling, and for Your promptness in my stumbling, I give You thanks, Lord.

SIMPLE TRUTH

God has never failed to keep an appointment.

SANCTUARY

*I will put my sanctuary
among them forever.*

EZEKIEL 37:26

FROM THE FATHER'S HEART

My child, throughout Scripture My people wanted to house My presence inside walls built by human hands. But it was only a symbol at best of My real presence which is with you always. I cannot be confined behind mortar or brick. Wherever My Spirit abides, there I am a sanctuary for hurting hearts. I am your sanctuary in the midst of your storms or in the celebration of your worship. In Me you will always find a safe place to hide.

A GRATEFUL RESPONSE

Lord, it was not just Your house, Your temple, Your church that became a sanctuary for worshipers. You, Yourself, are my Sanctuary. Wherever You are, I find peace and contentment. In Your presence I find a safe and permanent refuge, a holy place where I can rest and worship and live all of my days. Thank You for making my heart a sanctuary for Your use.

SIMPLE TRUTH

Home is a sanctuary, only if Jesus lives there.

JEHOVAH-NISSI—
THE LORD IS MY BANNER

Moses built an altar and called it
The LORD is my Banner.

EXODUS 17:15

FROM THE FATHER'S HEART

My child, the battles you fight in your heart are not new. All
of My children wage war at different times. But remember
I am your banner. When you hold up My name, every
enemy will flee. My banner over you will bring peace, victory, hope, and restored joy. Build an "altar" to Me in your
heart—spiritual stones of remembrance that remind you of
My faithfulness each time you experience a victory. My
banner over you will always be love.

A GRATEFUL RESPONSE

You are the name I lift up in times of temptation, Lord. You
are my Jehovah-nissi, my Banner, waving Your sovereign
authority clearly in view of all my enemies. When You are
present, victory always follows.

SIMPLE TRUTH

Hope comes not by looking at our own circumstances,
but by reviewing God's track record of faithfulness.

THE RAM

Abraham looked up and there in a thicket
he saw a ram caught by its horns.
He. . . sacrificed it as a burnt offering instead of his son.

GENESIS 22:13

FROM THE FATHER'S HEART

My child, I've always known My destiny. Throughout the Bible you will find the clues that lead you to My Father's heart. I tested Abraham's faith on the mountain that day, but I knew he would obey Me. Just as I didn't require his son for a sacrifice, I do not require a physical sacrifice from you. There is nothing you can do to pay for your sins. I only want you to turn away from your sin and let Me be that ultimate sin sacrifice. I was that ram that God provided—just in time. I gave My life for you.

A GRATEFUL RESPONSE

When I read of Abraham's willingness to sacrifice his son, I realize it was a picture of You, Lord. You, the innocent ram, stepped in, not just to save Isaac's life, but the lives of millions to follow—as many believers as there are stars in the sky or grains in the sand.

SIMPLE TRUTH

Faith does not look forward or backward; faith reaches upward.

SIMPLICITY

Jesus replied,
"Foxes have holes and birds of the air have nests,
but the Son of Man has no place to lay his head."

MATTHEW 8:20

FROM THE FATHER'S HEART

My child, sometimes your wants far exceed your needs. Things will never satisfy the depths of your soul. Only I can do that. Your heart yearns for simplicity, yet you do not always understand. Enjoy the things with which I have blessed you, but realize again only one thing is needful. Treasure our relationship. Let it influence every other relationship here on earth, and every decision or commitment you make. True simplicity is found as you seek after My heart.

A GRATEFUL RESPONSE

You had no home to call Your own, no place to lay Your head, no savings accounts, and no fancy wardrobes. If the Son of God could live in simplicity, why can't I? Truly You've shown that simple things are best: treasures of the heart that can never be measured monetarily but are remembered eternally.

SIMPLE TRUTH

Simplicity is not a "fad-i-tude," but an attitude of the heart.

COMFORTER

And I will pray the Father,
and he shall give you another Comforter,
that he may abide with you for ever.

JOHN 14:16 KJV

FROM THE FATHER'S HEART

My child, I know when your heart is breaking, when you've said good-bye to the last dreams of your heart. I'm here for you, and I will hold you as long as you need to rest in My arms. My Spirit is ever present as the Comforter to speak peace to your heart and soul. In every sorrow, and for every tomorrow, I will be there. No one else can make that promise to you.

A GRATEFUL RESPONSE

Lord, I never need to look farther than the comfort of Your arms. There You wait for me with expectant heart, longing for my fellowship. How many times I've felt Your strong arms and quiet whispers to my aching heart! Where else could I turn? Lord, You are my Comforter.

SIMPLE TRUTH

Just when we think all hope is gone, Jesus fills our
hearts with song.

THE GREAT PHYSICIAN

"I am the LORD,
who heals you."

EXODUS 15:26

FROM THE FATHER'S HEART

My child, rest in Me. I have given you a prescription for healthy living. When you allow your body to stress out and destructive emotions to run rampant, My healing cannot come. I am not only the mender of broken bones and dreams, but I am the restorer of broken hearts and lives. I am the great physician, and I care for all My patients with tenderness and love.

A GRATEFUL RESPONSE

Lord, I bring the pains of a wounded heart and the aches of a broken body to You. I feel Your personal presence surrounding me with quiet assurance. Your touch releases my pent-up emotions, and healing flows through me like a fountain. Lord, You are my great physician.

SIMPLE TRUTH

God's home is where we can hang our hurts.

HOSPITALITY

You prepare a table before me in the presence of my enemies.
You anoint my head with oil; my cup overflows.

PSALM 23:5

FROM THE FATHER'S HEART

My child, don't you know My heart is an open house for you? Just as you prepare a place for Me in your heart, I, too, have a heart that welcomes all My children. I've prepared the finest delicacies for you to eat. I love nothing better than to sit down with you at My table and enjoy sweet fellowship together. "Welcome Home" is something you will hear as soon as you step across the threshold of heaven. But even now, I extend hospitality to you. I have a big house—and a big heart. You are always My treasured guest!

A GRATEFUL RESPONSE

You roll out a carpet of clover and invite me to renew Your friendship daily in quiet, green meadows. As part of Your royal hospitality, You lay an extravagant table with a delicious feast, fit for a child of the King. My cup overflows with gratitude.

SIMPLE TRUTH

In a sense, we have been given the privilege of being the caretakers of another's happiness.

FATHER TO THE FATHERLESS

His name is the LORD. . . .
A father to the fatherless.

PSALM 68:4–5

FROM THE FATHER'S HEART

My child, no matter what your earthly father's limitations, I will make up for them. And when your dad has gone, you will not be a fatherless child. I am more than adequate to be the kind of father you always wanted. Some of My children had no father here. To them, I often give a double portion of My grace, just so they will know and feel My love surrounding them. I have a big family—and I love them all.

A GRATEFUL RESPONSE

To those who have no family, You whisper, "Come." You are Father to the fatherless, a hero for all times. And in heaven, sealed away forever, are the adoption papers, signed with Your own lifeblood. I'm so glad to be one of Your children. Every day should be my Father's day.

SIMPLE TRUTH

No matter where our journey takes us, God is the
friend that welcomes us back home, again and again.

BURDEN BEARER

Praise be to the Lord, to God our Savior,
who daily bears our burdens.

PSALM 68:19

FROM THE FATHER'S HEART

My child, how I love to carry your burdens! Your shoulders are much too weak to bear that weight. I should know. I created you for My glory, and with God-shaped needs. Like a loving father with his child, I welcome you into My arms the moment you run to Me. Let Me be a burden-bearing tree for you. Daily, hang up your worries and cares upon My branches. But don't forget to leave them there. I'll know what to do with them.

A GRATEFUL RESPONSE

I know my problems are only opportunities from You to help me grow. But when heavy loads weigh me down, You're there as my burden bearer. There's no problem too difficult for You to solve, and no burden too heavy for You to bear. Lord, I thank You for carrying me when I cannot walk.

SIMPLE TRUTH

Compassion is always in fashion.

CONSUMING FIRE

*For the LORD your God
is a consuming fire.*

DEUTERONOMY 4:24

FROM THE FATHER'S HEART

My child, I love you, but My love will not tolerate other
"gods" or "idols" in your heart. My holiness is like a consuming fire that burns through all the chaff of your life.
Always keep Me first in your life. Make every moment
count for Me. No, you cannot do it alone. But trust Me to
purify every motive and burn away every useless thought
until you emerge through the fire, pure as gold.

A GRATEFUL RESPONSE

Lord, my worthless deeds and thoughtless words are as
ashes in Your purifying fire. You've redeemed even the care-
less years, sparked by matches of rebellion. You are a consuming fire. But instead of destroying me with Your anger,
You've brought beauty out of ashes and consumed me with
Your love.

SIMPLE TRUTH

*The best test of character is what you do when no one
is looking.*

THOROUGHNESS

*Thus the heavens and the earth were completed
in all their vast array.*

GENESIS 2:1

FROM THE FATHER'S HEART

My child, I created nothing in the world without fore-thought. Do you really think any creature could just "evolve" without precise, delicate thoroughness from My hand? If I know when a sparrow falls, and how many hairs are on your head, do you not also believe I am in control of the details of your life? You were a child in My heart long before you were a spark in your mother's eyes. With thoroughness, I created the world and everything in it. And with thorough-ness, I will carry out My eternal plan for you.

A GRATEFUL RESPONSE

Lord, no detail escapes Your watchful eye. Every color, line, and shadow meet Your approval. Every blade, leaf, and petal exemplify Your work. Every muscle, tendon, and vessel work together in a crowning masterpiece of creation. I thank You for Your thoroughness.

SIMPLE TRUTH

God has no timetables to complete His work.

Day 172

MY CONFIDENCE

> *For you have been my hope,*
> *O Sovereign LORD,*
> *my confidence since my youth.*
>
> PSALM 71:5

FROM THE FATHER'S HEART

My child, when you look away from Me like Peter did in the water, you will sink every time. Confidence is not something you build up inside yourself. You don't find courage and confidence by gazing at your mirror reflection. Let Me be your mirror. Let Me be your confidence. Let My words fill your mind, heart, and spirit. Look up, not down.

A GRATEFUL RESPONSE

Lord, You turned a timid teenager into a blossoming creation of Yours. If anything good ever comes from this life, it will be because You have been my confidence. Your Word has given me strength to believe in myself. Your love has given me courage to pursue the dreams You gave. I owe everything to You.

SIMPLE TRUTH

Jesus loves us, just as we are becoming.

PROMISE KEEPER

*Not one of all the good promises
the LORD your God gave you has failed.
Every promise has been fulfilled.*

JOSHUA 23:14

FROM THE FATHER'S HEART

My child, promises mean nothing without fulfillment.
Others offer you balloon promises, filled with nothing but
hot air that vanishes at the first pressure point. But My
words will never fail. Examine them closely. Every promise
I have given you is yours to claim. What are you waiting for,
child? Believe Me today. I am your promise keeper. Will you
keep your promises, too?

A GRATEFUL RESPONSE

In a world where "I do" rarely means, "I'll keep my
promise," You shine as the ultimate promise keeper. You've
never broken a promise, and You've never been untrue. No
one else can claim that. Thank You for being true to Your
word, and true to Your name.

SIMPLE TRUTH

Each promise of God is a personal gift of hope.

SENSITIVITY

"Are not two sparrows sold for a penny?
Yet not one of them will fall to the ground apart from
the will of your Father."

MATTHEW 10:29

FROM THE FATHER'S HEART

My child, I will never turn away when you are hurting, nor will I heap on your shoulders more than you can bear. I'm sensitive to your pain, and I feel the deepest cries of your heart. You cannot fathom that I could care for millions and still acknowledge one of My children's needs. That's the kind of Father I am. And that's the kind I'll always be.

A GRATEFUL RESPONSE

Lord, I'm amazed at Your sensitivity. With the whole world's problems to consider—managing presidents and kings, mending broken lives, moving mountains, mopping up floods, to name a few—You still have time to care for the smallest of Your creations. And You have time for me. Thank You, Lord.

SIMPLE TRUTH

The test of true love is a servant spirit.

DISCERNER OF THE HEART

*For the word of God is quick, and powerful,
and sharper than any twoedged sword. . .
and is a discerner of the thoughts and intents of the heart.*

HEBREWS 4:12 KJV

FROM THE FATHER'S HEART

My child, do you fight a daily barrage of thoughts that try to distract you from My work and My mission for you? I know your heart. I can discern your truest motives before you utter a word. Think about Me and about My words to you. Submit every thought to Me. I will help you capture every unholy thought and turn your heart toward Me again. When you feed your heart with My spiritual food, an abundance of treasure will emerge.

A GRATEFUL RESPONSE

Lord, there is no way to hide from You, even if that were my desire. My thoughts are like a cinema screen, flashed before Your holy eyes. You are a discerner of the heart; You can see through every excuse I make or mask I wear. Thank You for knowing me so well, and still loving me so much.

SIMPLE TRUTH

*Be careful what you feed your mind. What goes in,
usually comes out.*

BREAKER

"One who breaks open the way will go up before them. . . .
Their king will pass through before them,
the LORD at their head."

MICAH 2:13

FROM THE FATHER'S HEART

My child, are you discouraged at times because of the evil you see around you? My enemies have assembled their troops and planned their strategies against Me ever since the beginning of time. And they will do the same to My children. But I am your breaker—your power source to blast through their rocky intentions. My name and power are a dynamo within you. And they are stronger than the forces that come against you.

A GRATEFUL RESPONSE

When I'm facing mountains too difficult to move, I remember Your promises to those who have gone before me. I've seen Your power as the breaker. Just as You delivered Israel, You are gathering Your people around the world to break through the evil and make Your name known.

SIMPLE TRUTH

There is no mountain too big for God to move.

CREDIBILITY

"Do not believe me unless I do what my Father does.
But if I do it, even though you do not believe me,
believe the miracles."

JOHN 10:37–38

FROM THE FATHER'S HEART

My child, examine My words. Test My promises. Read of My miracles. Then ask, believing I will answer. I have no agenda except what My Father has written for Me. If I acted on My own, there would be no credibility to My character. But My authority—and My assignment—comes from above. Believe in Me because He sent Me.

A GRATEFUL RESPONSE

Who in their right mind could deny Your power? Who could witness Your work and not believe? You have credibility, not because we say so, but because You mirror Your heavenly Father. You love as He loves, heal as He heals, forgive as He forgives. Lord, I don't need a miracle to know You are real.

SIMPLE TRUTH

Some people refuse to believe unless they see, and some refuse to see even when they do believe.

ALTOGETHER LOVELY

His mouth is sweetness itself;
he is altogether lovely.

SONG OF SONGS 5:16

FROM THE FATHER'S HEART

My child, you've looked for someone to capture your heart and bring you romance all of your life. Even those most precious to you on this earth will never satisfy you like I can. I am your lover, your friend, your groom, and your lifelong companion. Ours is a sacred romance, the kind whose affections will never die, because I have set My heart on you. I am altogether lovely and you, My child, are so beautiful to Me.

A GRATEFUL RESPONSE

Like a bridegroom awaiting my entrance, You are standing there, Lord, as I walk down the aisle. You are the most beautiful sight I have ever seen. Your eyes are full of truth. Your heart is pure as gold. Lord, You are altogether lovely. How I love You, Lord.

SIMPLE TRUTH

Love is always the right choice.

FOURTH MAN IN THE FURNACE

"Look! I see four men walking around in the fire,
unbound and unharmed,
and the fourth looks like a son of the gods."

DANIEL 3:25

FROM THE FATHER'S HEART

My child, never fear when you walk through fiery circumstances. An unexpected death, a wretched failure, a business loss, an unexplained illness—they will come like unwelcome flames in the night. Don't be terrified but look closely. In the middle of that fiery furnace, you'll see a familiar face. I'll walk through the flames with you.

A GRATEFUL RESPONSE

Before I even smell the smoke, You've already extinguished some fires. But other times I've walked through the flames, not knowing the outcome. Just as You were the fourth man in the furnace, Lord, for Daniel's friends, You have taken the heat for me—and my hair wasn't even singed.

SIMPLE TRUTH

When in doubt, faith it out.

APPROACHABILITY

*Come near to God
and he will come near to you.*

JAMES 4:8

FROM THE FATHER'S HEART

My child, I ripped away the chasm between your sin and the Father. Like a bridge over the Grand Canyon, My death and resurrection opened a path to My Father's love. I grieve when you pull away from Me. Enter boldly into My throne room day or night. You can always run home. Draw near to Me. I am approachable.

A GRATEFUL RESPONSE

You're the perfect parent, Lord, never pleading, "I'm too busy" or "Don't bother me now." Thank You for Your approachability, for letting me interrupt Your day with my petty thoughts and paltry dreams. Thank You that You're only a prayer away.

SIMPLE TRUTH

The best way to call God is person to person.

THE ANSWER

You answer us with awesome deeds of righteousness,
O God our Savior.

PSALM 65:5

FROM THE FATHER'S HEART

My child, does your heart still search for truth? Are you confused about the whys of life? Study My words. Let Me share with you the mysteries of My kingdom, available only to My children. I reward the diligent seeker, as I hold the keys to life. I'm waiting to unveil so many things I want you to know. I am the answer.

A GRATEFUL RESPONSE

A thousand questions pelt my life like the raindrops of a summer storm. Too often, after I've searched in vain, I finally turn to You. You not only have the answers I need, but You are the answer. Through nature, through Your Word, through the whisperings of Your Spirit, I hear You, Lord.

SIMPLE TRUTH

Even in changing times, God's faithfulness remains a constant source of help—ever loving, ever guiding, ever giving.

INTERPRETER OF DREAMS

Then Joseph said to them,
"Do not interpretations belong to God?
Tell me your dreams."

GENESIS 40:8

FROM THE FATHER'S HEART

My child, do you want to know if a dream is from Me? Weigh it in light of the principles in My Word, and you will know. What should you do about nightmares? Read My Word before bedtime, and it will flush out every fear. Whether your dream is conscious or subconscious, I care. Tell Me your dream, Child, and I'll tell you the dreams I've designed for you. I am the interpreter of dreams. Together we can accomplish great things.

A GRATEFUL RESPONSE

Lord, I know You spoke through dreams long ago. I know You are the only true interpreter of dreams because You are the only One who knows our every subconscious thought. You are the only One wise enough to do so.

SIMPLE TRUTH

When God changes your heart, He may change your dreams.

SINGLE-MINDEDNESS

*"My food," said Jesus,
"is to do the will of him who sent me
and to finish his work."*

JOHN 4:34

FROM THE FATHER'S HEART

My child, if someone claims you have a one-track mind, accept it as a compliment—if that means your mind, heart, and soul are centrally focused on Me. My single-minded mission from the beginning has been to do the will of My Father and nothing less. Others tried to distract Me, as they will you, but you must remain strong and protect our love at all costs. Just as I finished My work on the cross, I will finish the good work I started in you. I will not leave you alone.

A GRATEFUL RESPONSE

You allowed nothing or no one to interrupt Your mission, Lord. Thank You for Your single-mindedness. Even when Your friends and family attempted to sidetrack You from Your main goal, You persevered to the end. I am the benefactor of Your success. Knowing You are there gives my heart strength for the journey and grace for the task.

SIMPLE TRUTH

All God wants is the permanent key to your heart.

CONSOLATION OF ISRAEL

*He was waiting for
the consolation of Israel,
and the Holy Spirit was upon him.*

LUKE 2:25

FROM THE FATHER'S HEART

My child, I love to give comfort and consolation to My children. I guided My chosen people—the Israelites—through deep waters, fire, hunger, and drought. When they rebelled, I disciplined them and loved them back. When they lost their focus, I gave them direction. When they needed peace, I gave them My promise of an eternal Messiah. Do you think I will do any less for you? I am your consolation, too.

A GRATEFUL RESPONSE

So many waited and hoped for Your coming, Lord. In anticipation of relief, comfort, and freedom from years of exile and hopelessness, they watched—and God was true to His Word. You are the consolation of Israel, and You are my comfort and hope, as well.

SIMPLE TRUTH

The floods may come, but a rainbow always follows.

REDEMPTION

*"When these things begin to take place,
stand up and lift up your heads,
because your redemption is drawing near."*

LUKE 21:28

FROM THE FATHER'S HEART

My child, many will come and claim to be the Messiah during the last days. Terror will grip the hearts of people as the world tosses in confusion. Sights such as you have never seen will abound. But in the midst of all the turmoil, you'll see hope arrayed in white garments in the sky. At that point, look up—your redemption draws nigh. I will come for you in the twinkling of an eye. I am your redemption, and I could come today.

A GRATEFUL RESPONSE

Lord, I don't have Simeon's promise that my eyes will visibly see You. But earthquakes, wars, violence, and strange signs indicate Your time is soon. You are my redemption, Lord. My final flight to freedom rests in the Father's timetable. I look forward to Your coming.

SIMPLE TRUTH

Hope finds a home in the arms of Jesus.

Day 186

FREEDOM

*Now the Lord is the Spirit,
and where the Spirit of the Lord is, there is freedom.*

2 CORINTHIANS 3:17

FROM THE FATHER'S HEART

My child, freedom is what everyone wants, but few under-stand its meaning or responsibility. True freedom is not the absence of conflict, nor is it the release from authority. I came to bring you freedom: freedom from rules that would blind you to the truth; freedom from the past that would hold you its prisoner; and freedom to embrace the future and all I've created you to be. I am your freedom, and My Spirit will bring you the truth that frees you to love and forgive.

A GRATEFUL RESPONSE

We find true freedom when our past becomes a stepping-stone to a brighter tomorrow. Only then can we find con-tentment in making today its own reward. Freedom for You came not from adherence to past laws, or in release from persecution, but from an attitude of love. Wherever You are, Lord, I find freedom.

SIMPLE TRUTH

*Freedom is the privilege of pursuing and discovering
God's best for our lives.*

SHIELD

*He is a shield for all who
take refuge in him.*

PSALM 18:30

FROM THE FATHER'S HEART

My child, anytime you are in danger, run to Me for safety. I love to be your shield. I have provided you with every piece of armor you need—the helmet of salvation, the sword of the Spirit, shoes of peace, a belt of truth, and the shield of faith. But as your overall shield, I will protect you and absorb any stray darts or bullets that try to penetrate your spiritual armor. The next time you are attacked, send your enemies My way. I'll take care of them.

A GRATEFUL RESPONSE

Lord, my own weapons are like ancient tools, useless in today's wars. The battles may be more sophisticated and the schemes of warfare more intense, but Your strength is superior. You are like a bulletproof vest that covers my entire body, mind, and spirit. You are my shield, Lord. I rely on You.

SIMPLE TRUTH

*Where can we go but to the Lord? He gives new
strength within each heart.*

HEIR OF ALL THINGS

He has spoken to us by his Son,
whom he appointed heir of all things,
and through whom he made the universe.

HEBREWS 1:2

FROM THE FATHER'S HEART

My child, can you fathom what it means to share in My inheritance? Everything that belongs to My Father belongs to Me. He has allowed Me to share My glory with you, and to supply all your needs. I am heir of all things My Father ever created—and He created everything! But out of all that I own, do you know what I treasure most? You, My child. You are My greatest treasure!

A GRATEFUL RESPONSE

The birds of the air, the beasts in the field, the kingdoms on earth, the treasures in heaven—they all belong to You, Lord. You are heir of all things Your Father created. And to think that I am joint-heir with You! As Your child, I own an inheritance far greater than money.

SIMPLE TRUTH

You are God's prized possession.

BOLDNESS

*When Jesus had finished saying these things,
the crowds were amazed at his teaching,
because he taught as one who had authority.*

MATTHEW 7:28

FROM THE FATHER'S HEART

My child, I am not the author of fear. Though My life was threatened many times, I was never afraid. Even when death called Me, My life was not taken by My enemy. I willingly gave My life in exchange for you. With boldness and assurance I completed every task necessary for My mission. Many recognized My authority because of My Father's boldness in Me. Remember, when your knees are knocking, and your hands are trembling, My boldness is yours for the asking.

A GRATEFUL RESPONSE

Your words were like daggers that pierced the heart. One command quieted a hurricane or raised the dead. One discerning statement embarrassed and infuriated Your accusers. Your teaching confused the most intellectual. I praise You, Lord, for Your example of boldness.

SIMPLE TRUTH

When faith comes in, fear goes out.

Day 190

WORD

*In the beginning was the Word,
and the Word was with God,
and the Word was God.*

John 1:1

From the Father's Heart

My child, I will always be a mystery to you until the day I call you home to live with Me. I and My Word are the same, and before time began, I and My Father existed in the Word. That Word clothed itself in human form when I was born of a virgin and entered the world. When you read My Word, you are listening to Me. And I have so much to tell you! One day you will understand this mystery. I am the Word—and I am all you need.

A Grateful Response

Lord, I don't understand this mystery, how You've always been here from the beginning. You are the Word, and yet You are God. Every page of Holy Scripture points to You as the driving force behind all of nature, wisdom, and knowledge. You are my Word for the day, and for all times.

Simple Truth

God's Word is still the best-seller of all time.

PILLAR OF CLOUD

*By day the LORD
went ahead of them in a pillar of cloud
to guide them on their way.*

EXODUS 13:21

FROM THE FATHER'S HEART

My child, whenever you encounter an obstacle, remember, I have already provided a way around it or through it. Just like I led the Israelites on their journey to freedom, I will lead you. A cloud can bring gale force winds, provide a covering for extreme heat, or bring refreshing rain. But I am Lord of the clouds. I will be your pillar of cloud, leading you to safety. The next time you see a cloud on the horizon, don't fear the storm. Look closely, and you will see and feel My presence.

A GRATEFUL RESPONSE

Lord, Your path is not always the shortest, but it is always the best one for me. Although the sands of time may shift and temporarily hide Your footprints, You are a pillar of cloud by day for me. The waves of Your love refresh me as I follow Your leading. Thank You for guiding me wherever I go.

SIMPLE TRUTH

Walking with your head in the clouds is not always a negative.

Day 192

PRAISEWORTHINESS

*We will tell the next generation the praiseworthy deeds
of the LORD, his power, and the wonders he has done.*

PSALM 78:4–5

FROM THE FATHER'S HEART

My child, I am giving you responsibility as My disciple. If you
find buried treasure, do you hoard it for yourself or do you
share the good news with others? Every truth, gift, and blessing I have given you is like buried treasure. If you never use
those precious jewels, never polish them, never share their
wealth with others, they will tarnish in your heart and be of use
to no one. What I have done is praiseworthy. Go tell someone
of My love today. The future generation depends on you!

A GRATEFUL RESPONSE

Even if our voices were silent, the rocks would join all creation in singing praise to You, Lord. But I want those who
come after me to find me faithful, Lord. You are praiseworthy, and as long as I have breath, I will use every opportunity to tell of Your power and greatness. There is so much
to share. Where do I begin?

SIMPLE TRUTH

*May those who walk our paths find our steps easy to
follow.*

SEARCHER OF
HEART AND MIND

*"I the LORD search the heart and examine the mind,
to reward a man according to his conduct."*

JEREMIAH 17:10

FROM THE FATHER'S HEART

My child, do you often weary of the temptation to do wrong? I know you would like to sweep away every wrong desire that ever enters your mind. But these come to test and make you strong, to see if your foundation will stand. Don't give in. One day you will battle that will no more. But for now, submit every thought and action to Me. I am the searcher of your heart and mind, and I will gently help you, not condemn you. Trust Me for strength.

A GRATEFUL RESPONSE

Lord, how do I know whether my motives are pure all the time? You read me like a book. You know me completely, inside and out. That brings me both relief and reverence. Thank You for being a searcher of heart and mind, and for purging my reasons and thoughts. Let everything in me give glory to You, Lord.

SIMPLE TRUTH

Peace comes when we exchange our excuses for God's reasons.

JESUS

That at the name of Jesus every knee should bow,
in heaven and on earth. . .
and every tongue confess that Jesus Christ is Lord.

PHILIPPIANS 2:10–11

FROM THE FATHER'S HEART

My child, how I love to hear you speak My name. Do you understand the power involved in the name of Jesus? Because of My Father, when you use My name, demons scatter, enemies fall, thunder echoes, winds calm, rocks shout, and mountains move like pebbles in the sand. Speak My name and hearts melt, knees bow, and tongues sing music sweeter than any song ever sung. Heaven opens its storehouse of blessing when My children ask—and speak My name.

A GRATEFUL RESPONSE

There is no other name under heaven or earth that stirs such emotions inside of me—a whirlwind of praise, a flood of tears, a shower of gratitude. You are Jesus, and no word can express, no tongue can confess adequately, the glory, majesty, and honor of Your name. Jesus, Jesus, Jesus—there is indeed something precious about that name.

SIMPLE TRUTH

Jesus is the only name worth pursuing, the only name
worth honoring, the only name worth remembering.

ATTENTIVENESS

For the eyes of the Lord are
on the righteous and his ears are
attentive to their prayer.

1 PETER 3:12

FROM THE FATHER'S HEART

My child, My heart breaks when I see world religions still bowing to gods who cannot speak, idols who cannot feel, images who cannot help. My eyes are always watching you closely and My ears always attentive to you. I'm ready at any given moment to send My angels out to fight on your behalf and give you the answer you have sought according to My will. I cannot help the ungodly until they turn to Me. Then all of heaven is at their disposal, too. Speak, Child. I'm listening—and I care for you so much.

A GRATEFUL RESPONSE

Not a sound escapes my lips that You do not hear, Lord. Like an eagle watching her little ones, You eagerly await and watch for me to pray. You really listen and hear me when I talk to You. Thank You for Your attentiveness, Lord.

SIMPLE TRUTH

God works overtime, anytime, all the time.

THE LAST ADAM

So it is written:
"The first man Adam became a living being";
the last Adam, a life-giving spirit.

1 CORINTHIANS 15:45

FROM THE FATHER'S HEART

My child, do you often wish you had not been born with Adam's sinful nature? So do I. But from the beginning, I knew the last Adam would transform your nature from a creeping caterpillar to a shimmering butterfly. I am that last Adam, the One who came to deliver you from an impossible plight when no one else could. Because of Me, the old Adam nature no longer holds you in bondage. You are free, My child. Enjoy the fellowship of that freedom!

A GRATEFUL RESPONSE

Lord, I'm so grateful that this natural, earthly body is not the end. The first Adam represented our sinful lives. But You are the last Adam, the spiritual dynamo that carries me across the threshold of eternity. One day I won't struggle with temptations any longer. Because You came, I can live forever.

SIMPLE TRUTH

What a shame to have wings and never fly.

MAN OF SORROWS

He was despised and rejected by men,
a man of sorrows, and familiar with suffering.

ISAIAH 53:3

FROM THE FATHER'S HEART

My child, I do understand your pain. I could remove it all and never let you suffer in this life. How could you help someone mend a broken heart if yours has never shattered? How could you understand the fresh tears from a graveside if you never buried a loved one? How could you comfort a hopeless life when you've never descended into a tunnel of despair? I am the man of sorrows, and because I've been there—with more pain than you'll ever know—I truly understand. Run to Me, Child. Let Me wipe away your tears and hold you until the hurt is gone.

A GRATEFUL RESPONSE

Compared to You, Lord, what do I know of pain and suffering? You are the man of sorrows, and suffering is no stranger to You. Even Your closest friends left You in Your greatest moment of need. You chose to be a victim, so I didn't have to stay one. Thank You, Lord.

SIMPLE TRUTH

Sorrow stretches the heart so God can refill it with
His joy.

DISCIPLINE

*But Jesus often withdrew
to lonely places and prayed.*

LUKE 5:16

FROM THE FATHER'S HEART

My child, before any major works or accomplishments, there must come discipline. The runner in the race must prepare physically and emotionally, and the soldier must train diligently for battle. Likewise, My children must discipline themselves to be fit for My kingdom's work. I, too, knew the discipline of drawing close to My Father. Your body cannot handle the pressure of constant movement. Your mind needs to pause from fast forward, and your spirit needs quiet retreat in My presence. I'll help you, Child. Rest in Me.

A GRATEFUL RESPONSE

Lord, even You needed time alone, time to commune with Your Father, time to think, time to rest. And that took discipline. I, too, need that discipline and time alone with You. Like a tree planted by the water, my roots can then grow deep into the soil of Your love. Thank You for Your discipline.

SIMPLE TRUTH

The road less traveled is often the road traveled alone.

ONE AND ONLY

No one has ever seen God,
but God the One and Only,
who is at the Father's side, has made him known.

JOHN 1:18

FROM THE FATHER'S HEART

My child, you will experience many kinds of love in your lifetime—love for your parents, your children, your close friends, your mate, and even the unlovely and needy. But there is only one love like ours. I am your One and Only God—the lover of your soul, the One from whom all affection stems. Without Me you have no idea what love is about. One thing is needful, My child. Let Me always be your One and Only love.

A GRATEFUL RESPONSE

So many impostors have come in Your name, Lord, claiming to be the Christ. But You are God the One and Only. You are the only Christ. The gods of other nations pale and wither at the mention of Your name. You alone hold the secrets of heaven. And You are my one and only love.

SIMPLE TRUTH

There is no love sweeter, no relationship richer, no friendship deeper than the love of Jesus.

MY SUPPORT

*They confronted me in the day of my disaster,
but the LORD was my support.*

PSALM 18:18

FROM THE FATHER'S HEART

My child, in the midst of deep waters, I will draw you out. When lightning bolts of disaster strike your heart, I will repair the damage. In your distress you can call on Me, for I will be your support. The cords of death will not overwhelm you. When you feel everything around you shaking loose, take heart. Lean hard on Me. I'm here for you. I'll lift you up.

A GRATEFUL RESPONSE

Stormy winds can beat against me, but You, Lord, are my support. You pick me up when I fall, and You prop me up when I'm leaning. Against nature's force, I'm at Your mercy. I am not strong enough to make it on my own. But You, Lord, are always there, reaching for my hand. Thank You, Lord, for holding on to me.

SIMPLE TRUTH

You never know what faith can do until you step into the water.

SERENITY

*"In quietness and trust
is your strength."*

ISAIAH 30:15

FROM THE FATHER'S HEART

My child, deep below the turbulent ocean's depths is a region marked by silence and serenity. Likewise, nestled deep in the eye of the "storms" you face is a place of rest. For wherever I am, there you can find serenity. No matter what is going on in your life, regardless of the confusion around you, I never change. And I will give you that peace for the asking.

A GRATEFUL RESPONSE

Lord, Your serenity calms my spirit daily. In the quiet moments of my life, I find the strength to persevere. In the silent spaces of my heart where You speak, faith finds a resting place. Thinking of You chases every worry and fear away and brings peace in every situation.

SIMPLE TRUTH

*In the eye of the storm, God whispers peace to our
hearts.*

DEFENDER OF WIDOWS

His name is the LORD. . .
a defender of widows, is God in his holy dwelling.

PSALM 68:4–5

FROM THE FATHER'S HEART

My child, you may feel lonely at times, but you are never alone. Even the widow who has lost the love of her life will find comfort and love in My arms. I delight in defending and blessing those who know their need for Me—those who look daily to Me for every provision, those who have made Me the one true love of their lives. I can meet their needs—your needs—like no one else. Try Me and see. I am the defender of widows, especially those who are "widowed" from their own selfish desires.

A GRATEFUL RESPONSE

How beautiful to know You personally care for those who live alone! You are a defender of widows, the friendless, and all who do not live under the protection of one to care for them. Those who play havoc in the lives of these special ones are in for a rude surprise when You show up in their defense. Thank You, Lord, that You are with all of us daily.

SIMPLE TRUTH

Only doesn't mean lonely when God is on your side.

EL ELYON, GOD MOST HIGH

He who dwells in the shelter of the Most High
will rest in the shadow of the Almighty.

PSALM 91:1

FROM THE FATHER'S HEART

My child, when gusty winds blow around you, I'll make your foundation strong. I'll rebuild your courage and strengthen your might when everything goes wrong. I'll repair the broken places and fill the gaping holes. Your job is to live under the shelter of My wings. When you do that, I, the Most High God, will cast My shadow over you, and you will find blessed rest. Just because I love you, My child, I will do this.

A GRATEFUL RESPONSE

Like an eagle spreading its wings to shade her offspring, You spread Your arms and protect me. There, I rest under Your shadow, away from the scorching heat of the sun, protected from the eyes of stalking enemies. You are El Elyon, the God Most High. With You, I am safe.

SIMPLE TRUTH

Trust is knowing that God will allow into my life
only the things that will be for my ultimate good.

RESTRAINT

"What is this testimony that these men are bringing against you?" " But Jesus remained silent and gave no answer.

MARK 14:60–61

FROM THE FATHER'S HEART

My child, do you think I don't understand when words sting like barbed wire? I've seen you hurt after rejection, when others ridiculed you and called you reckless names. I've taken note of those who have teased you and tried to sway you from your belief in Me. But I've been there. I will give you wisdom and strength to remain steadfast. Just as I showed restraint, you can, too. In the end, your innocence will shine like stars in the night. Others will see—and believe.

A GRATEFUL RESPONSE

You knew the time for golden silence, Lord. When Your enemies demanded a response to their accusations, You uttered no idle words, no self-promotion, and no angry defenses. You were like a sheep led to slaughter. You knew Your mission, and You also knew Your divine status. Yet You remained selfless. I'm humbled by Your restraint, Lord. You are an example for me.

SIMPLE TRUTH

Love your enemies. They'll think you're crazy and leave you alone.

ETERNAL GOD

*Abraham planted a tamarisk tree in Beersheba,
and there he called upon the name of the LORD,
the Eternal God.*

GENESIS 21:33

FROM THE FATHER'S HEART

My child, you have no concept of the magnitude of eternity. How could you? Although I created you in My image, you are limited now by finite humanness. But I have put My Spirit within you. I have placed in your heart the longing for eternity—another world, another place. That way, you won't be so tied to this existence that you forget what eternity is for. I am your Eternal God, and I'm preparing you to dwell with Me forever.

A GRATEFUL RESPONSE

In my limited understanding I cannot imagine a place or a person where time has no limits. You are Eternal God. All of the greatness, goodness, and beauty in You I have come to know will never end. Right now I see only a tiny glimpse of You. You are forever, Lord, forever.

SIMPLE TRUTH

*Who would want to stay earthbound after a glimpse
of eternity?*

SOURCE OF STRENGTH

He will be. . .a source of strength
to those who turn back the battle at the gate.

ISAIAH 28:6

FROM THE FATHER'S HEART

My child, when you are discouraged and weary, don't give up. My grace is sufficient for your weakness. You may need physical rest, and that's good, for you must treat your body well, too. But you don't need to depend on your own energies to succeed. I am your source of strength. When you turn to Me, depend on Me, and let Me work through you, there is no need for defeat. You serve Me well, My child. Now let Me strengthen you.

A GRATEFUL RESPONSE

Lord, sometimes I feel like a tiny sapling, bending in the breeze, or a tired soldier trying to hold down the fort. But as I raise my spindly branches, and as I lift my aching arms toward the Son, You are my source of strength. You are growing me into a sturdy oak. Only You refresh me. Thank You, Lord.

SIMPLE TRUTH

We cannot quell the hunger in our souls with more
work or piety. Often what we really need is rest—
sweet rest in Jesus.

ORDERLINESS

God saw all that he had made, and it was very good.
And there was evening, and there was morning—
the sixth day.

GENESIS 1:31

FROM THE FATHER'S HEART

My child, remember that My children who have the gift of organization must help those who do not. But orderliness is more than mere organization. The orderliness of My character designed a plan from the beginning. I knew exactly what I was doing, and when I would do it. Nothing is haphazard in heaven. Are you struggling with perfectionism? Lighten up. Excellence is all I require. Feeling scattered? Let Me order your thoughts so that they stay focused on Me daily.

A GRATEFUL RESPONSE

Lord, You could have created everything in the world in one day or in one moment. You could have reversed creation and put man here first. But Your world is a world of precision, and everything was created according to your divine orderliness. Your wisdom is awesome.

SIMPLE TRUTH

Choose only those pursuits that strengthen your relationship with Him. Other things cry for your attention, but He wants to give you a heart devoted to Him alone.

RADIANCE OF GOD'S GLORY

The Son is the radiance of God's glory.

HEBREWS 1:3

FROM THE FATHER'S HEART

My child, in your darkest night I will always be a light for you. You can never escape My presence, for I will come and find you and bring you back to Me. I am the radiance of God's glory, and one day you will share that glory with Me in heaven. But until that day, let Me be your mirror so you can reflect the Father's radiance, too. You will find in Me your hope of glory.

A GRATEFUL RESPONSE

You, Lord, are the sun in the morning and the moon at night. You are a reflection of Your Father and the light in my dark world. Although I can't see God with my earthly eyes, I can see the brightness of heaven on the darkest day. You are the radiance of God's glory—and the joy of my life.

SIMPLE TRUTH

Home is where the lamp of God never burns out, and the Light of the World always shines in.

YOUR GREAT REWARD

"I am your shield, your very great reward."

GENESIS 15:1

FROM THE FATHER'S HEART

My child, do you understand all that I have planned for you? Everywhere you look, I have planted My blessings for you. Those who love Me will never be disappointed. Think of life as a treasure hunt, only let your search be for Me. Others look all their lives for meaning and purpose, but at the end of their rainbow there is no pot of gold, only heartache. When you search for Me, you will find great, abundant treasure. I am your very great reward.

A GRATEFUL RESPONSE

Lord, I need no wreaths or victory crowns. My life deserves no praise. You are enough, just to see Your face and to live in Your presence forever. You are my great reward. With thankful adoration, I can share in a royal celebration forever.

SIMPLE TRUTH

To see His face, His smile—a goal worthwhile.

NOBILITY

*"A man of noble birth went
to a distant country to have himself
appointed king and then to return."*

LUKE 19:12

FROM THE FATHER'S HEART

My child, I was born a peasant's birth, but My Father is a king. I borrowed a cattle's feed trough for My head, yet My Father owns the cattle on a thousand hills. I had no home of My own, yet My Father owns all the property in the world. I had no royal garments, yet I was clothed in My Father's righteousness. For you, I gave up kingship temporarily to be your Savior. I am nobility—and you are a child of the king.

A GRATEFUL RESPONSE

Lord, You gave us parables to help define Your kingdom and its work. Each one points to Your nobility. In Your kingdom You rule with love, and not with an iron fist. And to think that I am part of Your royal family! Lord, thank You for giving me Your nobility.

SIMPLE TRUTH

He extends His royal scepter, and to our hearts He says, "Come!"

GOD OF ABRAHAM, ISAAC, AND JACOB

"I am the God of your father, the God of Abraham,
the God of Isaac and the God of Jacob."

EXODUS 3:6

FROM THE FATHER'S HEART

My child, I have called out great leaders in the past—gifted men and women—who followed Me in faith throughout their lives. But I delight in using all My children. Yes, I am the God of Abraham, Isaac, and Jacob. But flaws dotted their characters, too. Still, I blessed them and used them. It's not how great your gifts are that determines how I use you, but how big your faith can climb and how available you are to Me. Remember, I'm a big God.

A GRATEFUL RESPONSE

Lord, I cannot stand in Your presence without shoes removed and heart bared. Wherever You are is holy ground. You are the God of Abraham, Isaac, and Jacob. How is it that a God this big, the God of these giants, could be my personal God, too?

SIMPLE TRUTH

When we look at ourselves, we see flaws. When God looks at us, He sees Jesus.

GUARANTEE OF
A BETTER COVENANT

*Because of this oath,
Jesus has become the guarantee of a better covenant.*

HEBREWS 7:22

FROM THE FATHER'S HEART

My child, the ancient priests held their positions because of
their tribal lineage. As long as they lived, they offered sacrifices as a condition of the Old Covenant. But when My
Father ushered in a New Covenant, He made Me a priest
forever—One whose blood would atone for all sin. I became
the guarantee of a better covenant, one that would bring
freedom from the penalty and power of sin forever. He did
that for you, Child—satisfaction guaranteed.

A GRATEFUL RESPONSE

Long ago I discovered how poorly I measured up to Your
laws, Lord. I couldn't go through a day without breaking at
least one. Yet, You came, the guarantee of a better covenant,
as the love sacrifice. Like a rainbow from heaven, You bring
hope and a way for new life.

SIMPLE TRUTH

> *In heaven no one will ever say, "I wish I hadn't
> followed Jesus."*

Day 213

WILLINGNESS

"The reason my Father loves me is that I lay down my life. . . .
No one takes it from me,
but I lay it down of my own accord."

JOHN 10:17–18

FROM THE FATHER'S HEART

My child, don't let anyone mislead you into thinking that I was a victim of a Jewish mob. My own people did not murder Me. I turned My life over to them willingly. I knew My Father's plan from the beginning—that I was born to die. And it is not your death I want, My child—only your life submitted to My will. I want a willing spirit that says, "I trust You, Lord, whatever You wish to do with my life." I promise you I have fantastic things in store for you.

A GRATEFUL RESPONSE

Lord, thank You for Your willingness to give Your life for me. You were not a statistic of Roman or Jewish executions. No one took Your life. You surrendered it of Your own free will. You placed Your life in the hands of murderers, just to give me life. That's some kind of love. How can I say thanks?

SIMPLE TRUTH

It is impossible to give yourself away—and not
receive something back in the process.

INTERCESSOR

We do not know what we ought to pray for,
but the Spirit himself intercedes for us
with groans that words cannot express.

ROMANS 8:26

FROM THE FATHER'S HEART

My child, bring Me your burdened heart often. You don't know what to pray? My Spirit, alive and well inside your heart, longs to pray through you. Bring every tear before My throne, for My Spirit knows and hears the unspoken words you long to utter. How precious to Me are the prayers of My saints. I am your intercessor, and I will hear every uncertain word, misguided thought, and confused question—and bottle them with your tears to present to My Father.

A GRATEFUL RESPONSE

Lord, when I have no words to say, You take my silent prayers and form a stairway to heaven, where God hears the deepest desires of my heart. In that sacred place known only to the Father, Your Spirit translates my longings into acceptable sacrifices. You are my precious intercessor.

SIMPLE TRUTH

Prayer opens heaven's doors.

PRINCE OF PRINCES

When they feel secure,
he will destroy many and take his stand
against the Prince of princes.

DANIEL 8:25

FROM THE FATHER'S HEART

My child, security is found nowhere except in the shelter of My Father's love and power. He has made Me the Prince of princes, stronger than the mightiest army—and you are under My charge and protection. While others look for safety in perishable places, you are different. A Prince knows His roots, His power, and His destiny. And He is not willing to lose one that has been entrusted to Him by the King.

A GRATEFUL RESPONSE

Lord, You are more powerful than all of the forces of evil, both visible and invisible. You are Prince of the princes. No one can stand against You, and one day, all eyes will turn and recognize Your power. One day every knee will bend beneath Your glory, and all wickedness will be destroyed. I worship You, Lord.

SIMPLE TRUTH

Jesus did not come to make room for Himself so that
He could rule the world. He came to rule in our
hearts so that we would make room for Him.

ENDURANCE

Consider him who
endured such opposition from sinful men,
so that you will not grow weary and lose heart.

HEBREWS 12:3

FROM THE FATHER'S HEART

My child, you're not the only one who's been rejected, wounded, and misunderstood for My sake. Remember My suffering and endurance, and let it encourage you when you feel like surrendering. I never intended for you to run the race alone. Not only is a cloud of witnesses hovering near—men and women of faith—but I'm standing at the finish line cheering you on. When you arrive, I have a crown just for you—the crown of endurance.

A GRATEFUL RESPONSE

Your endurance is my example, Lord. I've never sweat drops of blood. I've never been crucified. All along the road, hecklers, doubters, and schemers lined Your path. But You finished the race; You completed the task. You even loved Your enemies. How can I give up now?

SIMPLE TRUTH

The crown He gives will be my applause to Him.

EXALTED ONE

Let them praise the name of the LORD,
for his name alone is exalted;
his splendor is above the earth and the heavens.

PSALM 148:13

FROM THE FATHER'S HEART

My child, no matter where you look, you will find the splendor of heaven. In the sound of rushing waters, in the wake-up call of spring, in the heavens grand and glorious—there, beauty is visible. When trees clap their hands, rocks cry out their praise, thunder voices its approval, and above all, you, when you, My child, celebrate who I am, it pleases Me. I am the exalted One, and your praises are sweet to My ears.

A GRATEFUL RESPONSE

Lord, Your world is like an artist's canvas. You've painted in rainbow colors for all creation to enjoy. I see Your signature in every fragile butterfly and every fragrant garden. I join creation in praising You, Lord, for You are the exalted One. You alone are worthy of praise and honor.

SIMPLE TRUTH

The beauty of creation is God's signature of blessing
for our lives.

SON OF MAN

"I tell you, whoever acknowledges me before men,
the Son of Man will also acknowledge him
before the angels of God."

LUKE 12:8

FROM THE FATHER'S HEART

My child, I was often called Son of Man so others would
know that My divine roots allowed human grief. When
others need help, will they turn to you if you don't understand or feel their pain? You cannot be too heavenly minded,
but you can walk so high above the clouds that you fail to
see the needs of people below. Born of the Spirit, yet of a
virgin, I can identify with mortal flesh. I see others—and
you. You are the reason why I came to earth.

A GRATEFUL RESPONSE

You were the Son of God, yet You were the Son of Man. This
miracle, this mystery, confuses the wise and challenges the
skeptics. But how could You have known what it was like to
walk in my shoes and feel my hurts had You not been both
human and divine? Thank You, Lord, for understanding.

SIMPLE TRUTH

God saw the world at its worst and gave us His best.

BALANCE

*"But seek first his kingdom and his righteousness,
and all these things will be given to you as well."*

MATTHEW 6:33

FROM THE FATHER'S HEART

My child, you're struggling with balance—as all My children do. You may think you can do all things, but you can't without Me. When you make Me your first priority, you'll be amazed at what you and I can accomplish together. Throw away your agendas, your fears, and your busyness. Exchange them for My balance. Like the spokes of a wheel, all your activities will turn smoothly when you are connected to the hub—Me.

A GRATEFUL RESPONSE

Lord, I find no record of Your struggle with priorities. You treated all fairly, and Your life maintained perfect balance. You punched no clocks, wore no watch, and never tried to please everyone. You knew who You were and where You came from. You're truly a wonder.

SIMPLE TRUTH

Simple pleasures are the best. When God is here, who needs the rest?

THE ONE WHO CALLS YOU

*The one who calls you is faithful
and he will do it.*

1 THESSALONIANS 5:24

FROM THE FATHER'S HEART

My child, every day voices cry out for your attention. At times you don't know which way to turn. That's why I'm here for you. Listen to My voice. I am the One who called you, and I am the One who will order your steps daily. In My strength, not yours, you will find sweet rest and victory. The ones I call for greater service are the ones who listen— and respond. I'll be faithful to do the work. Your job is to obey.

A GRATEFUL RESPONSE

When work mounts up, and energy falls, You remind me of my calling, Lord. You are the One who called me and chose me before I ever knew Your name. You are the One who empowers me to do unexplainable things. And what You start, You always finish. Thank You for working through me to accomplish Your tasks.

SIMPLE TRUTH

The world has yet to see what you and God can be.

SEEKER OF THE LOST

*"For the Son of Man came to seek
and to save what was lost."*

LUKE 19:10

FROM THE FATHER'S HEART

My child, I love all My "sheep" the same. But if you strayed outside the gate, do you know what I would do? I would make sure the other sheep were secure for the night, and I would come after you. I would leave no stone unturned, no bush unsearched until I found you, folded you in My arms, and carried you back home where you belong. There are lost sheep all around you. Will you help Me find them and love them, too?

A GRATEFUL RESPONSE

I have been that lost coin, and I have also been the one sheep out of one hundred You found wandering outside the fold. You didn't write me off, kick me out, or lock the gate. You are a seeker of the lost. I'm so glad You looked for me and found me. Thank You for bringing me into Your fold.

SIMPLE TRUTH

While 10 percent loss of customers won't make or break most businesses, God spares no expense in trying to recover even one lost customer.

RESOLUTION

*As the time approached for him to
be taken up to heaven,
Jesus resolutely set out for Jerusalem.*

LUKE 9:51

FROM THE FATHER'S HEART

My child, how I long to reach into your heart and take those heaped-up fears and throw them into one huge bonfire! Some days, it's all you can do to pull back the covers and wash your face. The dread of another day drains your energies before you ever begin. But I have work for you to do—and blessings yet unclaimed. Just as I accepted My destiny with resolution and joy, you can, too. Set your face toward the Son and see those fears vanish.

A GRATEFUL RESPONSE

Walking into Jerusalem was like heading for the eye of the hurricane or approaching a hive of killer bees. You knew the fate that awaited You: certain betrayal and death. Yet, Your resolution to obey superseded the danger You faced. I can learn so much from You, Lord.

SIMPLE TRUTH

*Jesus desires more than our fellowship. He also wants
our "followship."*

OVERSEER OF YOUR SOULS

For you were like sheep going astray,
but now you have returned to
the Shepherd and Overseer of your souls.

1 PETER 2:25

FROM THE FATHER'S HEART

My child, look around you. Everywhere you go, I have provided green pastures for your food and restoration. I've out-
lined your boundaries and enclosed you all about with My
love. At the entrance I've placed My gate, so that no one can
touch you without first dealing with Me. I am your Shepherd
and the Overseer of your soul. No wolf in sheep's clothing
can destroy you. You are safe in My presence. Happy grazing!

A GRATEFUL RESPONSE

Lord, I can never stray farther than Your arms can reach.
You are the Overseer of my soul, standing guard and keeping watch like a Shepherd over His sheep. You know the
number of Your flock, and You call each of us by name.
Why would I want to leave Your lush pastures? How precious You are, Lord.

SIMPLE TRUTH

Our Overseer sees over us, around us, behind us, and
through us—and loves us anyway.

LAWGIVER

For the LORD is our judge,
the LORD is our lawgiver.

ISAIAH 33:22

FROM THE FATHER'S HEART

My child, My laws are not intended to rain on your party or hinder your freedom in any way. To the contrary, My laws bring freedom and protection. Can you imagine a civilization where every person does what is right in their own eyes? I've seen it. And believe Me, you don't want that. I am the lawgiver. Because there are rules, you know the boundaries. I love you far too much to allow you to make your own rules. Trust Me.

A GRATEFUL RESPONSE

When I was small, my parents gave me rules to follow, designed not for punishment, but for my own protection. You, Lord, are my lawgiver, and Your laws are perfect. They, too, are designed to keep me from harm. My heart wants to obey Your every word, Lord.

SIMPLE TRUTH

God's laws are not options to choose but commands to follow.

SOCIABILITY

On the third day a wedding took place at Cana in Galilee. . .
and Jesus and his disciples had also been invited to the wedding.

JOHN 2:1–2

FROM THE FATHER'S HEART

My child, I did not create you to live alone. All around you
I have placed divine appointments—people to love, people
with needs. Do you have room in your heart for others? Do
you know what to say when you walk into a crowded room?
Some are skilled in drawing out the best in others, while
others shrink in terror at the thought of speaking the first
word to a stranger. People need the Lord, My child. And I
need you to tell them about Me. I'll give you the words—
and sociability, too.

A GRATEFUL RESPONSE

Wherever people flocked together, Lord, You made room in
Your heart for them. Meeting needs, touching lives, changing hearts, You spent time with all of them, no matter what
their status, background, or race. Lord, if You loved and
needed people, so do I. Your sociability encourages me to
make others a priority. Thank You for caring.

SIMPLE TRUTH

Jesus' welcome mat is always out.

THE LIFE

"I am the. . .
truth and the life."

JOHN 14:6

FROM THE FATHER'S HEART

My child, living life to the fullest requires one thing and one thing only. I am the life—I am the One who designed you, formed you, and breathed My Spirit into you, and I sustain you. Apart from Me, there is no life. Because I am in your heart—because you have chosen to invite Me there—I can bring you true, abundant life. That's why I came. You won't find it any other place but in Me. Celebrate life, My child!

A GRATEFUL RESPONSE

Lord, You are life itself. Apart from You, I have no meaning. Without You, I am like a seed eternally dormant in the ground—never growing, never bursting forth into full bloom. But with Your life in me, I can blossom eternally. You are my life, Lord.

SIMPLE TRUTH

Where there are no roots, there is no life.

SERVANT

"I tell you the truth, no servant is greater than his master,
nor is a messenger greater than the one who sent him."

JOHN 13:16

FROM THE FATHER'S HEART

My child, do you want to be great in My kingdom? Do you long for more influence and greater boundaries? Do you want to touch more people? Then be a servant. Watch what I do. How have I loved you? How have I cared for you? How have I humbled Myself? Do the same. Ask Me to bless you. I'll send you someone whose feet and heart need washing. I was a servant. I'll make you one, too.

A GRATEFUL RESPONSE

One of the things I love about You most, Lord, is Your servant's heart. You stripped away Your kingly robe, and from Your pool of blessing, You washed my feet, my hands, my head, my heart. You sought no accolades. You humbled Yourself even to death. You are truly a servant, Lord. Keep giving me baths, Lord! I want to be just like You.

SIMPLE TRUTH

If you find yourself thinking someone needs a bath,
think again. They probably just need you to wash
their feet.

SUPREMACY

*So that in everything
he might have the supremacy.*

COLOSSIANS 1:18

FROM THE FATHER'S HEART

My child, everything I have done and everything I am point to My supremacy. I am the One who orchestrates the hands of Congress; I am the One who turns the hearts of leaders. I am the One who established My church. I am the One who created all things. I am the One who once destroyed the world by flood; I am the One who defeated every wicked army. And I am the One who loved you so much that I died for you—to become your supreme Lord.

A GRATEFUL RESPONSE

Lord, Your name, Your reputation, Your heritage, Your nature —all demand the respect and honor of Your subjects. You have supremacy, Lord. My home is Your castle; my heart is Your home. My worship belongs to You alone.

SIMPLE TRUTH

Jesus' supreme sacrifice on the cross settled the question of God's love forever.

MY PORTION

You are my portion, O LORD;
I have promised to obey your words.

PSALM 119:57

FROM THE FATHER'S HEART

My child, do you know how much your obedience blesses Me? Just like an earthly parent, I love to hear you say, "Yes, Father." Do you know I love to say "yes" to you, as well? I love to bless My children—wonderfully, completely, extravagantly. Let Me be your portion—the One you value above all others. Daily, let's fellowship and share our love together.

A GRATEFUL RESPONSE

Of all the things I treasure most, You are my most prized possession, Lord. Like a river of hope running through my life, You are my portion and my inheritance, a continual blessing each day. Lord, I need nothing but You.

SIMPLE TRUTH

If all your earthly possessions were removed, would
Jesus be enough?

ATONING SACRIFICE

This is love: not that we loved God,
but that he loved us and sent his Son
as an atoning sacrifice for our sins.

1 JOHN 4:10

FROM THE FATHER'S HEART

My child, when the high priest entered the holy of holies, he would make atonement for the sins of the nation. Once a year, the blood-sprinkled altar would testify to the atoning of sin. But I became the atoning sacrifice for all time—the once and for all lamb offered on your behalf for your sins so you could have life. I loved you first—so that you could love Me back. But even if you didn't, I'd still love you. I'd still die for you.

A GRATEFUL RESPONSE

Where once was offered a lamb or a goat, a sacrifice needed for sin, You became the atoning sacrifice. Your blood, shed on the cross, covered my sin forever. You were the sweet sacrifice, poured out with love, so that I could find a home in the heart of God.

SIMPLE TRUTH

To find God, let your heart do the walking.

URGENCY

*"As long as it is day,
we must do the work of him who sent me.
Night is coming, when no one can work."*

JOHN 9:4

FROM THE FATHER'S HEART

My child, don't let a single day go by without meeting Me here. You need My strength and power to accomplish the work I've chosen for you. There are many I want to bless through you, and time is so short. Since life is but a vapor, I want you to treasure each moment I give you. I'll be coming back soon. Until then, stay faithful to your calling. Let My urgency transform your desires. I can't wait to give you your next assignment.

A GRATEFUL RESPONSE

Every moment was a precious jewel in Your hands, Lord. You had only three years to accomplish Your mission. Diligently, faithfully, and obediently, You worked to train, teach, and disciple. My life is the result of Your urgency. Thank You, Lord.

SIMPLE TRUTH

Don't divert—stay alert!

RIDER ON THE WHITE HORSE

I saw heaven standing open
and there before me was a white horse,
whose rider is called Faithful and True.

REVELATION 19:11

FROM THE FATHER'S HEART

My child, when I come back for the final battle on earth, heaven's armies will surround Me. I will come riding on a white horse, and victory will adorn every banner you see. Take heart, My child. For a little while you will experience the pangs of a sinful world, and the daily struggle will seem like anything but a victory. But I am here with you now, and one day I will appear—and destroy evil for good.

A GRATEFUL RESPONSE

Like the roar of rushing waters, like the explosion of a volcanic eruption, You are coming back again, Lord. You are the rider on the white horse, my true prince in shining armor, followed by Your armies of faithful warriors. Violence, cruelty, injustice, and death will all be swallowed up in You. You are Lord indeed.

SIMPLE TRUTH

No Prince Charming ever promised so much—and
delivered it all—like Jesus.

PILLAR OF FIRE

Neither the pillar of cloud by day
nor the pillar of fire by night left its place
in front of the people.

EXODUS 13:22

FROM THE FATHER'S HEART

My child, you will face danger repeatedly. Obstacles will line your path. Darkness will obscure your view. Terror will stalk you like a lion on the loose. But I am your pillar of fire to guide you through. I will blaze a trail for you that will tunnel through every mountain, burn through every forest, and clear every cloud. Stay close to My side. There, the smoke won't get in your eyes.

A GRATEFUL RESPONSE

Even when I can't see a thing in front of me, there You are, Lord, blazing a trail as a pillar of fire. Just as You led the Israelites out of bondage by Your own raging forest fire, You send Your protection out ahead of me. Lord, I can't go wrong following You.

SIMPLE TRUTH

Some fires give warmth, light, and comfort; others
destroy everything in their paths.

FORESIGHT

*"Before I formed you in the womb I knew you,
before you were born I set you apart."*

JEREMIAH 1:5

FROM THE FATHER'S HEART

My child, I know you intimately. I always have. Nothing you've ever done is a surprise to Me. With great foresight, as I designed all of creation, I planned the lives I wanted you to touch, the paths I wanted you to take, the gifts I wanted you to use for My glory. I set you apart to be My special treasure. Yes, you. Your life is far more valuable than any of My creations. I make no mistakes. I love you, My child, with an undying love.

A GRATEFUL RESPONSE

Lord, did You really know everything about me long before I was born? My hair color, my eyes, my size, my mistakes, my successes, my needs? You had such foresight in Your creation. Everything fits together, just like You planned. You're amazing, Lord.

SIMPLE TRUTH

What we achieve depends on our relationship with the One in whom we believe.

JEHOVAH-MEKODDISHKEM, THE LORD SANCTIFIES YOU

That ye may know that
I am the Lord that doth sanctify you.

EXODUS 31:13 KJV

FROM THE FATHER'S HEART

My child, all of your straining to be perfect will profit you nothing. It is impossible for you to keep every one of My laws. You cannot make yourself holy by doing anything. It is My blood shed for you that makes you holy. And as your Jehovah-mekoddishkem, it is I who will continually sanctify you and conform you to My image. Rest in Me, child. I know your heart's desire is to please Me. That's what I want. Keep our relationship close. I'll do the rest.

A GRATEFUL RESPONSE

Sometimes I feel like Peter, Lord, when You were washing his feet. I need to wash Yours instead. But You are Jehovah-mekoddishkem, the Lord who sanctifies, the One who washes me continually with Your own blood. You are continually working in my life to make me holy.

SIMPLE TRUTH

No tree ever bore fruit by saying, "I think I can, I think I can."

RIGHTEOUS ONE

*"They even killed those who predicted
the coming of the Righteous One."*

ACTS 7:52

FROM THE FATHER'S HEART

My child, there is none righteous but one. I am the Righteous One, the God who longs to give My goodness to every person I've created. Those who accept Me and follow Me, I will clothe with My righteousness, just as I have done for you. No longer is there a barrier between you and heaven's gates. Our relationship, My child, is based on My righteousness—and your acceptance of it. I'm so glad you're My child!

A GRATEFUL RESPONSE

Through the years people have tried to tarnish Your name—and the names of those who knew You. But You are the Righteous One, Lord. You are the only One worthy enough to be called "Good." Next to You, Lord, my goodness is like muddy water. Thank You for accepting me as I am.

SIMPLE TRUTH

*God is not so concerned about whether we fall. . .but
whether we get up again.*

DEMONSTRATIVENESS

But God demonstrates his own love for us in this:
While we were still sinners, Christ died for us.

ROMANS 5:8

FROM THE FATHER'S HEART

My child, how do I define love? Love is who I am. Love is
what I did for you. Love is how I will always treat you. I
chose to let you know how very precious you are to Me by
dying for you. Is there any greater love than this? It didn't
matter what you looked like, or what you had done. I
demonstrated My love so you would know without any
doubt My words are not empty. When I say, "I love you," I
mean it, My child. Will you demonstrate your love for Me
by letting Me love through you today?

A GRATEFUL RESPONSE

You didn't just say You loved me, Lord. You showed me.
Though I felt like a broken piece of discarded pottery, You
treated me like a piece of fine china. Your demonstrative-
ness, Lord, Your love in action, won me over. As I love You
in return, You are the one who changes me.

SIMPLE TRUTH

The miracle of God's love is not that He loves us—but
that He loves us as we are.

ENABLER

He makes my feet like the feet of a deer,
he enables me to go on the heights.

HABAKKUK 3:19

FROM THE FATHER'S HEART

My child, come with Me as I take you on an imaginary journey. We are walking up a high mountain, and the path is very rocky. Take My hand; I won't let you fall. A few more steps—here we are at the top. Now, My child, I want you to walk back down by yourself. I'll be beside you, but you must use the faith feet I have given you. I am your enabler, no matter what rocky heights you encounter. I've given you hinds' feet—you were made for adventures like this. Trust Me. You'll be amazed at the extraordinary feats you can accomplish with My enabling strength.

A GRATEFUL RESPONSE

Upon the rocky mountain slopes You set my spirit free. With angel wings You lift me higher than I've ever been and plant my feet on solid ground once again. Thank You, Lord, for being my enabler, the One who pushes me beyond my ordinary limitations.

SIMPLE TRUTH

Hope begins when our strength ends.

DIRECTOR OF MY PATHS

In all thy ways acknowledge him,
and he shall direct thy paths.

PROVERBS 3:6 KJV

FROM THE FATHER'S HEART

My child, do you want to be successful? Really successful? Do you want to discover My plans for you? Then make My ways known. Wherever you go, wherever I lead you, let others know whose you are, and who I am. Nothing is impossible to those who believe in Me. I love to give you wisdom and to chart your course for you. I am the director of your paths. Listen for My voice telling you, "This is the way. Walk there." You can trust your Father's voice. I'll never lead you astray.

A GRATEFUL RESPONSE

For charting the course, for designing the dreams, for renewing Your promises daily—a thousand thanks of gratitude go to You, Lord. You are the director of my paths. You alone will remove the obstacles in the road so I can find safe passageway on my journey.

SIMPLE TRUTH

Three reasons to trust God: (1) He is faithful; (2) He
is faithful; (3) He is faithful.

INITIATIVE

We love because
he first loved us.

1 JOHN 4:19

FROM THE FATHER'S HEART

My child, when I saw the product of My special design—the day you were born—I was overjoyed. Did you know I "danced" at your birth? I loved you then, but in fact, I loved you long before you entered your mother's womb. So much did I want our fellowship and love relationship to be secure that I died for you, rose again, and began filling you with blessings from day one. In fact, I have chased you with blessings—so you would love Me, too. The day you said "I do" to Me was a happy day for Me.

A GRATEFUL RESPONSE

Before I even knew Your name, You loved me, Lord. It didn't matter what I looked like, or where I'd been. Even in my "unloveliness" You took the initiative and loved me first. I don't understand why You did that for me. How could anyone resist a love like that?

SIMPLE TRUTH

Genuine love doesn't need a reason to express itself.

JUDGE

And the heavens proclaim his righteousness,
for God himself is judge.

PSALM 50:6

FROM THE FATHER'S HEART

My child, there is nothing you can do to win My favor. I am not an ogre who waits to criticize your every move. I am the judge, but you are not under condemnation. I want no bribes, no sacrificial deeds of appeasement. Why would I need them? I own the cattle on a thousand hills. I am wealthy beyond measure. Everything is Mine. What matters to Me is your attitude, and our relationship, based on faith. I will judge the wicked, not you.

A GRATEFUL RESPONSE

I need not tremble before the Father's throne, although there is nothing good in me. Jesus, You will plead my case. And because of Your death and sacrifice, my sentence has been dismissed. You are my judge, Lord. Thank You for declaring me innocent.

SIMPLE TRUTH

Tolerance is the ability to lay aside our differences for
the greater cause of unity.

YIELDEDNESS

Yet it was the LORD'S will
to crush him and cause him to suffer.

ISAIAH 53:10

FROM THE FATHER'S HEART

My child, others stomp on your "rights" constantly and challenge you to react in unbecoming ways. In those moments, remember My pain. Remember that My Father's will included suffering and the yielding of rights. My "yieldedness" gave you a pattern in dealing with others—and opened up throne rights for all of My children. I exchanged My rights for God's best. Can you do the same?

A GRATEFUL RESPONSE

If You, the Son of God, were crushed, stricken, afflicted, and oppressed with no rights of Your own, should I expect to be treated any differently? In exchange for my past, You offered Your throne. In exchange for my rights, You made heaven my home. Lord, thank You for Your "yieldedness."

SIMPLE TRUTH

There are no career ladders in heaven.

THE ONE ENTHRONED
ON HIGH

Who is like the LORD our God,
the One who sits enthroned on high,
who stoops down to look on the heavens and the earth?

PSALM 113:5

FROM THE FATHER'S HEART

My child, heaven may seem far away, but it is as near to you as your heart. I am the One enthroned on high, but I don't live in palaces. I live in the hearts of all My children. I am not too high and mighty to overlook the down and out. Every child of Mine will one day sit at My table where a luscious feast has been prepared in their honor. Yes, I have many rooms in heaven, but they are all under one roof—My roof, and My love. When I come again, we will live on high forever.

A GRATEFUL RESPONSE

Although Your home is in heaven, You always take time for each of Your creations. Gently and tenderly, You nourish them, breathing new life and beauty into each one. You are the One enthroned on high, but You live in my heart, as well. Lord, thank You for caring for one like me.

SIMPLE TRUTH

His royal decree of love can never be reversed; we are
His children forever.

GIVER OF GOOD GIFTS

"How much more will your Father in heaven give good gifts to those who ask him!"

MATTHEW 7:11

FROM THE FATHER'S HEART

My child, I get so excited thinking up all the surprises I'd like to send your way. Gifts. Wonderful blessings to enrich your life. There's so much I want to do for and through you. But there's a catch. You limit Me, My child. Come, sit a while, and tell Me your heart's desires. You have not because you do not ask. Trust Me to take every desire and wrap it in the way I know will bless your life the most. Wait until you see what I've planned for you today.

A GRATEFUL RESPONSE

Whatever You give, Lord, is good and perfect. You wrap each gift with tenderness, adorn it with love, and tie it up with ribbons of blessing that fill my days with heaven's best. Nothing that comes from Your hand is a mistake. You are the giver of good gifts. And I receive You gladly.

SIMPLE TRUTH

The best things in life are found in Jesus.

IMMORTALITY

Now to the King...immortal...
be honor and glory for ever and ever. Amen.

1 TIMOTHY 1:17

FROM THE FATHER'S HEART

My child, one day your closet will no longer need reorganizing. You can throw your old clothes away. No more temptation to stuff it with things you won't wear. When that time comes, you will be clothed in immortality like I am. You will wear your eternal robe of righteousness. I am immortal—and together we will live forever.

A GRATEFUL RESPONSE

When You've completed Your purpose for my life, Lord, I will pass from death to life. I will enjoy Your immortality, like a butterfly taking flight from its cocoon. You give me wings to fly, Lord. When that time comes, I can soar to my heart's content. And I will praise You, My immortal King, with all my heart.

SIMPLE TRUTH

It's hard to put on new clothes when you keep wearing the old ones.

WATCHMAN

*The LORD watches over
all who love him.*

PSALM 145:20

FROM THE FATHER'S HEART

My child, you can relax in My arms. I'm much more capable of protecting you than you are yourself. Are you terrorized by the events you see in My world? A thousand may fall all around you, but I will keep evil from your home. I am your watchman, and I have eyes in the back, front, and on the side! I can see in every direction what's coming your way. Nothing escapes My attention. Continue on faithfully, My child. I'm in control.

A GRATEFUL RESPONSE

Just like a faithful security guard, wary of every surrounding detail, You keep watch over my life. I trust You, Lord, for You see before me and behind me. In daylight or dark, from every direction, I feel Your awesome protection. Thank You for being my watchman.

SIMPLE TRUTH

*We are never out of sight or out of mind. God's love
and light reach farther than the eye can see.*

AWARENESS

"You see the people crowding against you,"
his disciples answered,
"and yet you can ask, 'Who touched me?'"

MARK 5:31

FROM THE FATHER'S HEART

My child, no matter how large My world grows, and no matter how many children I have, there is room in My heart for every one of them. I especially hear the cries of My hurting children and feel the touch of faith from those who press through to reach My heart. I want all to come to Me, and none to perish. I am aware of every heartfelt need, every devastating pain, every crushing blow you face. Reach out and touch Me, My child, and I will make you whole.

A GRATEFUL RESPONSE

You see my face, speak my name, and touch my life, even among a thousand other people. How is it that You, who care for so many, still have time for me? Your awareness of those around You amazes me, Lord. You are such a personal, loving God.

SIMPLE TRUTH

When we travel, we see landmarks. When Jesus traveled, He saw faces.

INDUSTRIOUSNESS

*"My Father is always at his work to this very day,
and I, too, am working."*

JOHN 5:17

FROM THE FATHER'S HEART

My child, I know you grow weary of the ordinary. Day after day the tyranny of urgency calls you to complete your given tasks. But faithfulness brings its own reward. My Father, always industrious, never ceases to work in the hearts of His children. I, too, am industrious, as I work through all My children. Take heart, My child. Your work matters. Let Me restore the joy of your kingdom work. Let Me be your power source of industry.

A GRATEFUL RESPONSE

Lord, You never cease from Your labor of love. You have always been at work in my life and in the world, long before I even knew You. How grateful I am that You value me enough to complete Your work in my life. Thank You, Lord, for Your industriousness.

SIMPLE TRUTH

God gives us all the time we need to do all the things we need to do.

FIRSTFRUITS

But Christ has indeed been raised from the dead,
the firstfruits of those who have fallen asleep.

1 CORINTHIANS 15:20

FROM THE FATHER'S HEART

My child, each time you walk into the hospital room of a loved one near death, sadness creeps in, and tears fill your eyes. I love your sensitive heart. Never forget that I died so that you and your loved ones—those who know and love Me—would not fear this moment. I died, but I rose again, the firstfruits of resurrection for all My children. In death, your loved ones—and you—will walk through that tunnel of death to a greater light, the light of My presence. And one day, you will have a totally resurrected body—just like Mine. Weeping is brief, but joy comes in the morning.

A GRATEFUL RESPONSE

Like the very first lily pushing through the earth's crust, You were the firstfruits of death, Lord. You are living proof that death has no victory, and the grave has no barriers. Because of Your resurrection, fear of death has no hold on us anymore. I praise You, Lord, for eternal life.

SIMPLE TRUTH

Death is but a crossing from winter to spring.

PRECISION

*There is a time for everything,
and a season for every activity under heaven.*

ECCLESIASTES 3:1

FROM THE FATHER'S HEART

My child, waiting is hard for you sometimes, isn't it? All good things come to those who wait for Me. You are anxious about many things, but you can trust My precision. As long as there is life and breath, there will always be seasons. And as long as I rule the world—which is forever—you can count on My perfect timing in your life. All things are beautiful in their time—even you, My child, especially you.

A GRATEFUL RESPONSE

Spring waters the parched ground. Summer's sunshine wraps each flower with a warm coat. Each golden leaf falls as if on cue, and nature waits with hushed voice, as You seal winter with a kiss of sleep. Thank You for Your precision, Lord. You're always on time.

SIMPLE TRUTH

Trust holds on. . .when fear lets go.

SAVIOR

*"And we know that this man really is
the Savior of the world."*

JOHN 4:42

FROM THE FATHER'S HEART

My child, it was for you I died—you and the whole world.
I came to rescue the ones lost in their own world of suffering and meaningless confusion. I came to open blind eyes,
long closed to the truth. I came to open the gates of prisoners whose hearts were hardened by hatred. I am the
Savior of the world, and whoever believes in Me for their
salvation will never die. But I am also your personal Savior,
continually freeing you from strongholds that threaten our
fellowship.

A GRATEFUL RESPONSE

Lord, You walked into my prison of darkness and broke the
chains that had bound me for years. You are not just my
Savior. You have released prisoners from fear and shame for
centuries. All power and might belong to You—my Savior,
God, redeemer, and friend.

SIMPLE TRUTH

*Who in their right mind would want to reenter
prison after tasting freedom?*

BLESSED ONE

*Again the high priest asked him,
"Are you the Christ, the Son of the Blessed One?"*

MARK 14:61

FROM THE FATHER'S HEART

My child, I am the Blessed One, and I long to share My blessings with you. Come to Me daily and ask for My hand to empower and fill you until you are like a well of spring water that overflows and splashes on others. Don't be afraid of My blessing. Whatever extraordinary things I ask you to do, I will always give you the strength and resources to do them. Just ask.

A GRATEFUL RESPONSE

Lord, Your precious promises appear like desert oases of blessing. You are the Blessed One, the One who deserves our praise. You have drenched me with showers of blessing. Now, I bless You. For the beauty of the earth, for Your magnificent creation, my heart gives You praise, Lord, and a standing ovation.

SIMPLE TRUTH

The one who multiplies what God has given always gains more.

THANKFULNESS

Then Jesus looked up and said,
"Father, I thank you that you have heard me."

JOHN 11:41

FROM THE FATHER'S HEART

My child, guard your heart against any spirit of pride or ingratitude. Remember that everything you own is a gift from Me on loan. In everything you must give thanks, even the things that tear at your heartstrings. I work all things out for My good, and your thankful spirit releases My power to do that. My Father deserves My gratitude because I could do nothing apart from Him. Thankfulness is a virtue I see in you. I'm thankful you are My child.

A GRATEFUL RESPONSE

Your attitude was one of gratitude, Lord. Like a clear reflection in a crystal lake, You mirrored the Father and stole no credit for Yourself. You even thanked Him before He answered. Your humble thankfulness is an example for me, Lord. Because of You, I see the Father.

SIMPLE TRUTH

Gratitude is giving God applause, for who He is and what He has done.

DESIRED OF ALL NATIONS

" 'I will shake all nations,
and the desired of all nations will come,
and I will fill this house with glory,'
says the LORD Almighty."

HAGGAI 2:7

FROM THE FATHER'S HEART

My child, may I share My dream with you? I have a dream that all nations will come to know Me and let Me fill their homes, hearts, and governments with My glory and grace. Another, My enemy, seeks the opposite: to tear as many away from Me as possible. But those who know Me are secure in the relationship we share. One day all will bow to My rule. Pray that other hearts will come to know Me as you do, Child.

A GRATEFUL RESPONSE

The world longs for the treasures of light, love, liberty, and life. You are the treasure God sent to earth. You, Lord, are the desired of all nations. You are the only One who satisfies every desire, every hope, and every dream that my heart can inspire. Lord, I desire You with my whole heart.

SIMPLE TRUTH

Love each nation as part of God's creation.

JEHOVAH-SABAOTH, THE LORD OF HOSTS

This hath been by your means:
will he regard your persons?
saith the LORD of hosts.

MALACHI 1:9 KJV

FROM THE FATHER'S HEART

My child, in your strength nothing is possible. At My command, a thousand angels would rush to your defense if I so desired to send them. I am Jehovah-sabaoth, the Lord of hosts. Nations who trifle with My affections and refuse My plans will reap the consequences. But those who follow Me have a winning army on their side. I will protect you, My child. Never fear.

A GRATEFUL RESPONSE

Lord, You have shown me that falling is not always failing. You pick me up and rescue me when I am overwhelmed. You are Jehovah-sabaoth, the Lord of hosts, a tower of strength for me. I have no other place to run to, no other shelter in which to hide. I depend on You, Lord.

SIMPLE TRUTH

When God is beside us, we need no one besides Him.

RESPLENDENCE

You are resplendent with light,
more majestic than mountains rich with game.

PSALM 76:4

FROM THE FATHER'S HEART

My child, have you looked at My world lately? I mean, really looked? My world reflects the beauty of heaven. My resplendence—the light of My presence—is all around you. How can anyone say there is no God? I have written My signature wherever you see beauty. I've done this so that you—and everyone—will know who I am. I want you to reflect My beauty, too.

A GRATEFUL RESPONSE

I can still remember the breathtaking view as I stood on top of one of Your highest mountain peaks, Lord. I could see radiant beauty in all directions. But You are far more beautiful. Brighter than the sun itself, Your resplendence is dazzling to my eyes. Jesus, how You shine!

SIMPLE TRUTH

When we are in touch with beauty, we are in touch with the Creator.

ONE GREATER THAN SOLOMON

*"And now one greater than
Solomon is here."*

MATTHEW 12:42

FROM THE FATHER'S HEART
My child, if I told you I would grant anything you wanted, what would you ask Me for? Solomon could have had wealth, health, or fame, but he asked for wisdom. So I gave him all of the other things, as well. But even with his incomparable wisdom and wealth, I am greater than Solomon. No one can surpass My wisdom. I created you—I know what's best for you—but I will give you wisdom if you ask. And My wisdom is unlike any you'll ever know.

A GRATEFUL RESPONSE
The wisest man on earth held only a fraction of Your wisdom, Lord. You are the One greater than Solomon. You hold together the wisdom of the ages, and all of the world's knowledge would be but a thimbleful compared to what You know, Lord. How wise You are!

SIMPLE TRUTH
Success is not how much you know or where you have been. Success is the character God has formed within.

LIVING ONE

"I am the Living One;
I was dead, and behold I am alive for ever and ever!
And I hold the keys of death and Hades."

REVELATION 1:18

FROM THE FATHER'S HEART

My child, when all great leaders have died, their claims to a better life, one filled with peace and prosperity, were buried with them. But I am the Living One. I am the only One who conquered death and rose again. No one stole My body. Hundreds of witnesses verified My resurrection. I'm alive, Child! And I love living in the hearts of all My children.

A GRATEFUL RESPONSE

You have journeyed to the center of death and back. Like nature awakening from a long winter's nap, You rose again—in three days. While others still look for the grave to open, I know You are the Living One. Lord, You live in my heart forever.

SIMPLE TRUTH

Jesus is the One who won over death.

DEPENDABILITY

*"The Father loves the Son
and has placed everything
in his hands."*

JOHN 3:35

FROM THE FATHER'S HEART

My child, are you ready for more responsibility? Are you ready for Me to enlarge your area of influence? As you prove faithful in small things, I will give you more to handle. My Father entrusted Me with His plan for the world. My dependability is an example for you, My child. If I ask you to do anything beyond your resources, it is so that you will trust Me to work through you and give Me glory. When you're ready, just ask. I'll stretch your abilities—and your territory.

A GRATEFUL RESPONSE

There was no job too hard for You to complete, no responsibility too difficult for You to handle, no burden too heavy for You to bear. God entrusted His power, love, nature—His all—into Your hands, Lord. Because You have dependability, I trust You with my life.

SIMPLE TRUTH

It only takes one—plus Jesus.

ADONAI, THE LORD

"Not everyone who says to me, 'Lord, Lord,'
will enter the kingdom of heaven,
but only he who does
the will of my Father who is in heaven."

MATTHEW 7:21

FROM THE FATHER'S HEART

My child, some people recognize Me only as a man, while others see Me as simply a Savior. But I long to be the blessed controller of their lives. I want to be Lord, Adonai, in every heart. When I am on the throne of your heart and home, there is peace and safety there. I will help you with all the other priorities in your life. I will help you do My will. Trust Me as your Adonai.

A GRATEFUL RESPONSE

One day with You is better than a thousand in the palaces of kings. You are my Adonai, my Lord and Master. You call my name, and a flood of joy overflows. You command my life, and a fountain of confidence takes over. You are my Lord, and I praise You today.

SIMPLE TRUTH

His lordship demands our all—nothing more,
nothing less.

THE ROOT OF JESSE

In that day the Root of Jesse
will stand as a banner for the peoples;
the nations will rally to him,
and his place of rest will be glorious.

ISAIAH 11:10

FROM THE FATHER'S HEART

My child, I love using ordinary people. It gives Me great delight to take the weak things of the world to confound the wise. Look at David, a shepherd boy destined for a king. And I, too, was born as an ordinary baby. As the Root of Jesse, David's father, however, I was of royal lineage. And as the Son of God, My roots connect earth to heaven—so you can blossom into a beautiful flower as My child.

A GRATEFUL RESPONSE

From an ordinary family, You brought an extraordinary king. I can trace Your human family tree back to royalty, Lord. You were a king in heaven, and You were in the lineage of a king on earth. You are the Root of Jesse, and Your branches reach all the way to this heart of mine.

SIMPLE TRUTH

Whom are we to call ordinary, what God has destined
for extraordinary?

CAUTIOUSNESS

Jesus warned them sternly,
"See that no one knows about this."

MATTHEW 9:30

FROM THE FATHER'S HEART

My child, I know you grow impatient sometimes with the delays in your life. You long to know the future, and how you fit in. Trust Me implicitly. Just as there is a time for every season and every activity under heaven, there is a right time for you. I exercised cautiousness in order for God's perfect plan to evolve. Would you settle for anything less than My best for you? Don't get in a hurry. Time is on My side.

A GRATEFUL RESPONSE

Just like that blind man whose eyes were opened, I'd cry out, "I was blind, and now I see!" But You exercised cautiousness, Lord, so no one would interfere with Your Father's plan. You knew the right time for the butterfly to emerge from the cocoon. You never let ego or pride sway You from Your task. Instead, You waited for Your Father's instructions. You are so wise, Lord.

SIMPLE TRUTH

How you handle today will determine what you are
tomorrow.

Day 263

LORD OF THE HARVEST

*"Ask the Lord of the harvest,
therefore, to send out workers into his harvest field."*

MATTHEW 9:38

FROM THE FATHER'S HEART

My child, I know you want to reach other people for Me.
At times the task is overwhelming, and you may feel ready
to surrender. Remember, you cannot accomplish anything
alone. I am the Lord of the harvest. It is I who draw others
to Myself, but I use workers like you to do it. Wait for My
power before you go out. And pray for more help. I'll tug at
the hearts of those who have been preparing all their lives
for such a call. Prayer works, My child. Prayer works.

A GRATEFUL RESPONSE

Just as the earth yields its golden harvest, waving an offering
of thanksgiving to You, so I wave my banner, my testimony
of faith to those around me. You are Lord of the harvest,
drawing in precious grain. Lord, thank You for letting me be
one of Your workers.

SIMPLE TRUTH

*Prayer reaches the hearts of those too far away to
touch.*

THE WORD MADE FLESH

The Word became flesh
and made his dwelling among us.

JOHN 1:14

FROM THE FATHER'S HEART

My child, I baffled the world when I entered as a baby born of a virgin. Who but God would think of such a marvelous plan? His words, wrapped up in precious cloths of grace— sent to a manger as the greatest treasure heaven could find. I was that Word made flesh. And I am your treasure for all time. I feel the same way about you.

A GRATEFUL RESPONSE

Lord, You entered the world not on a white horse or wrapped in kingly robes. You came as an innocent baby, the Word made flesh. What a precious way to begin Your life on earth! Your Word has been fleshed out in my life, too. You, who were once a baby, have now become my living Lord.

SIMPLE TRUTH

No one but God could send His only Son so you and I
could experience His priceless work of heart.

INTELLIGENCE

The Jews were amazed and asked,
"How did this man get such learning without having studied?"

JOHN 7:15

FROM THE FATHER'S HEART

My child, all the degrees in the world will not make you more like Me. But I have given you the mind of Christ, and I expect you to use that mind to its fullest capacity. Meditate on My words daily. Others were astounded at My intelligence because I spoke My Father's words. When your time comes to speak, trust Me. Don't rely on your own intelligence, or you will fail every time. Open your mouth, and I will fill it with My words.

A GRATEFUL RESPONSE

Those who listened to Your words found no Ph.D. following Your name. You were taught at the knee of Your Father. You spoke not Your own words, but the words of God. Lord, I praise You for Your intelligence.

SIMPLE TRUTH

Lord, teach us to open the doors of our minds, and
shut the doors of our mouths.

JEHOVAH, THE SELF-EXISTENT ONE

God also said to Moses, "I am the LORD [Jehovah]."

EXODUS 6:2

FROM THE FATHER'S HEART

My child, I think by now you are aware of My awesome power, My jealous nature that demands allegiance and obedience, and My holiness that cannot look upon sin. I am Jehovah, the self-existent One, the One who hung the world on its axis and gave life its beginning. But I am also the Jehovah God who chooses to fellowship with you. My covenant is for you, My child, and all those who will choose to let Me fellowship with them. That covenant is irrevocable.

A GRATEFUL RESPONSE

All of creation looks to You for their beginnings. Before any creature walked the face of the earth, You were there, Lord. You are Jehovah, the self-existent One—the God who first initiated a covenant with man. You, Lord, are all I need.

SIMPLE TRUTH

We can never truly comprehend that an awesome, holy God could love us. We can only accept it.

BUILDER OF THE TEMPLE

And he will branch out from his place
and build the temple of the LORD.

ZECHARIAH 6:12

FROM THE FATHER'S HEART

My child, you cannot confine My glory to a temple, though
many have tried to do so. My power will break through the
walls and reach into the hearts of people who receive Me. I
am building a greater temple than Solomon's, or the one
Nehemiah rebuilt. I'm in the process of building a new temple—made up of believers everywhere—where My glory
will be housed permanently in a New Jerusalem. You're one
of the stones!

A GRATEFUL RESPONSE

Human hands have not drawn the blueprints for our final
home, Lord. You are gathering Your people as living stones
to build the temple of God. You, Lord, are the builder of the
temple. I'm so glad You chose me to be a part of Your long-
range building plans.

SIMPLE TRUTH

Sticks and stones may break our bones, but love, God's
love, will heal them.

FIRMNESS

Your statutes stand firm;
holiness adorns your house for endless days, O LORD.

PSALM 93:5

FROM THE FATHER'S HEART

My child, though your enemies try to shake you to the core, you can stand firm. Because I am with you, you need never stumble or fall. I am rock solid, and I will be your firm foundation when everything else is crumbling around you. Give Me your hand and hold on tight. Together we can withstand any "earthquake."

A GRATEFUL RESPONSE

I have not built my faith on sinking sand or crumbling rocks. Your Word, Your very nature, has firmness, Lord. And as long as I plant my life in the center of Yours, I can stand confidently. Lord, You and Your Word will never end.

SIMPLE TRUTH

When the only place we can look is up, He is faithful
to meet us and greet us at our point of need.

COVERING

Blessed is he whose transgressions are forgiven,
whose sins are covered.

PSALM 32:1

FROM THE FATHER'S HEART

My child, sin leaves you exposed to all kinds of catastrophes—like trudging through a blizzard in shorts or walking through hot coals barefooted. But My death, My blood, and My love form a covering for you. No longer can the sins of the past haunt you. Live in My joy and freedom and in My covering of love and forgiveness. My favor rests on those who have asked—and received—My forgiveness.

A GRATEFUL RESPONSE

Lord, You send a blanket of love, like new-fallen snow, to cover my life parched with sin. As time goes by, You melt each flake, never stopping to look underneath the covers. Soon blossoms appear where nothing grew before, as You replace the desert with springtime. You are my covering, Lord.

SIMPLE TRUTH

Is there a safer, warmer place to be than beneath the covering of God's arms?

HORN OF MY SALVATION

*He is my shield
and the horn of my salvation.*

PSALM 18:2

FROM THE FATHER'S HEART

My child, where can you find strength but in Me? Where do you look for safety but in Me, the horn of your salvation? If you trust in yourself, you will fail. If you look to others, you'll fail. Let Me surround you with My songs of deliverance. When I'm finished with your enemies, you'll feel like dancing and praising again!

A GRATEFUL RESPONSE

I am like a pebble in the shadow of Your mountain, Lord. I am but a midget, but You are the giant. You are the horn of my salvation, and in You I find anointing and power for whatever work You assign me. I praise Your strength, Lord.

SIMPLE TRUTH

*Never a moment or day goes by but Jesus is always
waiting nearby.*

LIBERALITY

*"You may ask me for anything in my name,
and I will do it."*

JOHN 14:14

FROM THE FATHER'S HEART

My child, giving is what I love to do. Will I give you everything you ask for? No. Did your parents? But I wait daily at your door to hear you call on My name and ask, so that your joy may be full—so you can bring glory to My Father. My liberality knows no bounds. Just look at what I did for you on the cross. Grace, mercy, and compassion are new every morning—these are but a small part of your daily "blessings box." Don't be afraid to ask, My child. I know what is best for you.

A GRATEFUL RESPONSE

Lord, I never need to beg like a dog at its owner's table. Neither do I want to misuse my inheritance to hoard up riches. You have given me Your name, an eternal credit card to use before the Father with Your blessing. Thank You for Your liberality. You have blessed me more than I could possibly deserve.

SIMPLE TRUTH

*Those who come to Jesus with empty hands will leave
with full hearts.*

PEARL OF
GREAT PRICE

*"When he found one [fine pearl] of great value,
he went away and sold everything he had and bought it."*

MATTHEW 13:45

FROM THE FATHER'S HEART

My child, most people search all of their lives for happiness.
But those who look for fulfillment in Me will find a treasure
far more valuable than any riches. I am the pearl of great
price, the one thing you cannot do without. Some "things"
may bring you temporary satisfaction, but I am the only
One who can satisfy your heart.

A GRATEFUL RESPONSE

You are worth more than all the silver and gold mines of the
world, all of the richest minerals, all of the wealth found in
the ocean's depths. You are the pearl of great price, the dis-
covery of a lifetime. I'm so glad I found You.

SIMPLE TRUTH

When you have Jesus, you have it all.

EL-SHADDAI, THE ALL-SUFFICIENT ONE

"I am God Almighty;
walk before me and be blameless."

GENESIS 17:1

FROM THE FATHER'S HEART

My child, everything your heart will ever need, you will find in Me. I am sufficient for every crisis. I am enough to heal your hurts. I am El-Shaddai, a God who dreams impossible dreams—and accomplishes them through My believing children. I love to show My might and power to a disbelieving world, just like I did through Abraham and Sarah. Everything is possible with Me. Do you really believe that, My child?

A GRATEFUL RESPONSE

Like a kitten whimpering to nurse its mother, I cry out to You, El Shaddai. You are my All-Sufficient One in a world of empty dreams. You are God of the impossible. You are God Almighty, who supplies my every need. You fill me up, Lord. Where would I go if not to You?

SIMPLE TRUTH

When God designs the dream, He will also direct the course.

PROPHET

*"Surely this is the Prophet who
is to come into the world."*

JOHN 6:14

FROM THE FATHER'S HEART

My child, every day is a miracle from Me. And I am constantly performing miracles in the lives of those who believe. But don't be like My people in the past who believed Me only because of My miracles. They remembered the prophets of old and the amazing works I did through My servants. But I am the Prophet sent by My Father to change hearts and lives forever—just like I have changed yours. Keep believing—not because of what I do, but because of who I am.

A GRATEFUL RESPONSE

The world awaited Your coming, Your salvation, and Your message. You are the Prophet, fulfilled through Scripture since the beginning of time. When You speak, people listen because You always tell the truth. I rejoice at Your coming. I celebrate Your work in my life. My heart will never be the same again.

SIMPLE TRUTH

The true Prophet always told the truth.

BENEVOLENCE

Praise the LORD. Give thanks to the LORD, for he is good;
his love endures forever.

PSALM 106:1

FROM THE FATHER'S HEART

My child, there's no need to hoard My blessings. Fresh mercy is available to you for the asking. Goodness is My inherent character. My love and benevolence last forever. If I went about doing good, so can you. If My love was extravagant, not stingy, so must yours be. No, you can't do it without Me. But if you'll keep coming to Me as an empty vessel, I'll fill you up and pour you out. I'll shine My love and goodness through you.

A GRATEFUL RESPONSE

Lord, You never contradict Yourself. And even when I don't understand the way You work, and sometimes question Your decisions, You can never act in any way but out of love toward me. You will never stop loving me. Thank You for Your benevolence, Lord.

SIMPLE TRUTH

Sin may crimp the flow of God's blessings temporarily,
but it will never cut off the Father's love for His child.

REPAIRER OF BROKEN WALLS

*"You will be called
Repairer of Broken Walls."*

ISAIAH 58:12

FROM THE FATHER'S HEART

My child, all My children suffer "breakdowns" in their walls at
one time or another. Those gaps in your armor where sin has
broken through, those tears in your heart that thoughtless
actions ripped away, those tornadoes that whipped through
your life without a warning—I've seen them all, My child. But
I am the Repairer of Broken Walls—and that includes your
heart. Renovation is My specialty. I'm always gentle but thor-
ough. Give Me your heart daily. I'll do the rest.

A GRATEFUL RESPONSE

Just like the broken-down walls of Your beloved city Jerusalem, my life had been broken beyond repair. Yet You took
the remains and mended the damage, restoring what was
destroyed. You are the Repairer of Broken Walls, and because of You, I now stand complete. Thank You, Jesus.

SIMPLE TRUTH

*Time alone never truly heals. Only the Father's touch
can restore completely what was lost.*

JUSTIFIER

For all have sinned and fall short of the glory of God,
and are justified freely by his grace
through the redemption that came by Christ Jesus.

ROMANS 3:23–24

FROM THE FATHER'S HEART

My child, sometimes I see you trying to strain for My approval like a child acting out to get his parent's attention. Your activities, busyness, and good works add nothing to our relationship unless they are done because of your love for Me—and not to earn My favor. I am the justifier, who made you pleasing in My Father's eyes, not because of your performance, but because of My death.

A GRATEFUL RESPONSE

How could I measure up to a holy, righteous God as You? I fall short, again and again. Yet because of Your love and grace, You are the justifier—treating me as if I had never sinned. Because of Your death, every sunrise is a brand-new day to welcome with joy.

SIMPLE TRUTH

God's thoughts never change toward His children.
Day by day, He showers us with new mercies,
unlimited grace, and unending love.

ENERGY

*He will not
grow tired or weary.*

ISAIAH 40:28

FROM THE FATHER'S HEART

My child, does your heart lack "get up and go"? Is your faith anemic? Do your knees buckle each time I call on you for a special task? Are you approaching emotional burnout? Cease your striving. You'll wear out if you don't. Wait on Me. Let Me empower you. My supernatural energy will keep you going and going and going.

A GRATEFUL RESPONSE

When light streams through my window, and morning calls too soon, You remind me that You are my strength, Lord. Your energy becomes mine, as we plan the day together. You're what keeps me going, Lord.

SIMPLE TRUTH

*In the arms of God, we'll find a resting place, a refuge
for our weary hearts. In His love He'll walk beside us,
holding our cares gently in His hands.*

LIGHTNING

"For the Son of Man in his day will be like the lightning, which flashes and lights up the sky from one end to the other."

LUKE 17:24

FROM THE FATHER'S HEART

My child, I write My name on the clouds with lightning strokes. My glory can be seen even in the storms. And just as My signature brightens the heavens, the very mention of My name will light up your heart with joy. One day all will watch as I return. As quickly as a lightning flash, I'll come for My bride. Soon, My child. It could be today.

A GRATEFUL RESPONSE

With lightning strokes, You walk across heaven, demanding the attention of all Your creation. And each one groans, longing for the day when You will light the skies with Your lightning return. Your signs are everywhere, Lord. I anticipate Your coming.

SIMPLE TRUTH

One glimpse of His face will tell us it has been worth the wait.

HUSBAND

*"For your Maker is your husband—
the LORD Almighty is his name."*

ISAIAH 54:5

FROM THE FATHER'S HEART

My child, I created you with a vacuum that could only be filled by Me. Earthly relationships, as wonderful as they seem, are but miniatures of the real thing. They can't satisfy all your needs or wishes. I am your husband and long always to be the first and only real love of your life. I'm planning a trip for My bride that exceeds anything you can even imagine—an eternal honeymoon in heaven!

A GRATEFUL RESPONSE

Lord, I can never truly be widowed, for You are my husband. You are the protector of my life, and priest of my home. You are a companion, friend, partner, lover, and spiritual leader. Everything I need in a husband, I find in You. Thank You for loving me.

SIMPLE TRUTH

There's no place like His presence.

PERCEPTION

The LORD knows the thoughts of man;
he knows that they are futile.

PSALM 94:11

FROM THE FATHER'S HEART

My child, whatever you think about in your heart determines what kind of a person you are. Ask daily for My perception. Every negative thought is like a poisonous pill that feeds your circulation with defeat. Let My thoughts penetrate your heart and soul so that you can keep heaven on your mind.

A GRATEFUL RESPONSE

As I bring each thought to You, Lord, You shape it into a beautiful flower. You know the deepest things in my heart, and only with Your mind can I think about things that are pure, lovely, and of good report. Thank You for Your perception, Lord.

SIMPLE TRUTH

Each day brings new celebrations to mind as we trace
the threads of His faithfulness and love.

MAN FROM HEAVEN

*And just as we have borne
the likeness of the earthly man,
so shall we bear the likeness of the man from heaven.*

1 CORINTHIANS 15:49

FROM THE FATHER'S HEART

My child, have you looked in the mirror lately? What do you see? Do you know what I see in My mirror? I see a precious child created in My image, bearing My likeness. Like a proud father, I love to boast, "My child looks like Me!" As you grow more and more in love with Me, I'm making you more like Me, the man from heaven—your heavenly Father.

A GRATEFUL RESPONSE

Lord, is it possible one day that I'll really look like You? To have my Father's eyes and my Father's love—this is my desire. You are the man from heaven, the One I admire, the One I'm looking forward to seeing in person.

SIMPLE TRUTH

No matter what people tell you about yourself, God knows—and loves—the real you.

REVELATION

*The revelation of Jesus Christ,
which God gave him to show his servants
what must soon take place.*

REVELATION 1:1

FROM THE FATHER'S HEART

My child, are you curious about the future? Does your heart feel any dread at the thought of coming events? Let Me comfort you, because I am the revelation. My Father controls the future, and you need not fear when you know Me. He has revealed much of life's final episodes through My testimony and the words of My faithful servants. You don't need to understand everything. What is required is that you love Me with all your heart, and that you're ready for My coming.

A GRATEFUL RESPONSE

Lord, You did not abandon us in some deep cave shrouded in mystery. Future events are not left to chance but are well planned in the Father's mind. You, Lord, are the revelation—showing us God's nature, reputation, will, and our future. Thank You for including me in Your future.

SIMPLE TRUTH

Tomorrow is never a question when God is in control.

LEADERSHIP

Do not be discouraged,
for the LORD your God
will be with you wherever you go.

JOSHUA 1:9

FROM THE FATHER'S HEART

My child, when others question you in your hour of trial—
"Where will you find a job now?" "What are your plans?"
"Why did this happen?" "Can you really do that?"—here is
how you can respond. Say these words: "My Father knows
the answers. And I trust His leadership. No matter where I
go, or what He asks me to do, I know He will be with me.
I'm not afraid because my leader is trustworthy. He will never
leave me alone." It will strengthen their faith—and yours.

A GRATEFUL RESPONSE

Following You has never been easy, Lord, but it has always
brought rewards. Thank You for Your leadership, for walking the path before me. Even when the load gets too heavy
to bear, for the rest of the way, You carry me there.

SIMPLE TRUTH

God will never lead you where His angels cannot keep
you.

REDEEMER FROM THE LAW

But when the time had fully come, God sent his Son. . .
to redeem those under law,
that we might receive the full rights of sons.

GALATIANS 4:4–5

FROM THE FATHER'S HEART

My child, the law is the law. But My grace is. . .My grace. And it's sufficient to fulfill what the law could never do. The law told you the right thing to do, but My redeeming grace empowers you to accomplish it. By yourself? Not a chance. But that's why I came to earth as your redeemer: to give you full ownership in the kingdom of heaven and to move beyond the law to full-fledged grace living and joy-filled giving.

A GRATEFUL RESPONSE

I was weary of the struggle between right and wrong, Lord. Aren't laws made to be broken? But You entered the scene, a bright light in the shadows, to do what the law could never do. You adopted me as Your own, forgave me, and empowered me to choose right. You are the redeemer from the law.

SIMPLE TRUTH

Grace gives me the freedom to be who God designed me to be.

AVENGER

O LORD, the God who avenges,
O God who avenges, shine forth.

PSALM 94:1

FROM THE FATHER'S HEART

My child, abandon your senseless inner weapons. You cannot fight injustice by warring in your spirit. Vengeance is Mine; I am the avenger. I am well prepared to defend My children. What I allow to be removed, I will restore, and if not in this lifetime, the next. Your part is blessing—not cursing—your enemies. Let Me avenge My own—and My children's honor. I know the final chapter of history because I wrote it.

A GRATEFUL RESPONSE

My heart cries out against injustice. Whether in my own life, those around me, or ones I've never met, senseless violence and injuries to heart and mind beg for avenging. You, Lord, are the avenger. And I trust Your timing.

SIMPLE TRUTH

Hatred robs tomorrow of its triumph—and gives
victory to the past.

IMAGINATION

How many are your works, O LORD!
In wisdom you made them all.

PSALM 104:24

FROM THE FATHER'S HEART

My child, did you know I had dreams, too? Who do you think designed every four-footed creature, every flower petal, and every winged insect? Who hung the stars in space and hollowed out the ground? Who raised the earth until it loomed majestically toward the sky in snow-covered brilliance? And who wrote the prescription for your eyes, hair, body shape, and gifts? My imagination lets Me dream big dreams, and My power accomplishes them. All things are possible through Me, My child.

A GRATEFUL RESPONSE

You wrap the mountains in a coat of majesty and sprinkle the earth with heaven's manna. You dot the night skies with Your magnificence, reminding me of my insignificance. You paint the earth with a multitude of rainbows. Lord, I love Your imagination.

SIMPLE TRUTH

The wonder of God's creation is surpassed only by the beauty of His love.

THE FIRST AND THE LAST

> *"Do not be afraid.*
> *I am the First and the Last."*
>
> REVELATION 1:17

FROM THE FATHER'S HEART

My child, have you been with Me so long and still wonder about My character? My power and holiness frighten you at times, but you need not fear. I love your reverential awe of Me, which tells Me you recognize weakness and powerlessness in yourself apart from Me. I am the First and the Last. No one came before Me, and no one will come after Me. What I say goes. I have always longed for everyone to become My child. But only a few hear and respond. I'm glad you did.

A GRATEFUL RESPONSE

Who can understand Your beginning or ending? You are not a figment of someone's imagination. You are not the result of a big-bang explosion. You are the First and the Last; You've always existed—from the beginning. Though I don't understand, I honor You, Lord, and bow at Your feet in wonder.

SIMPLE TRUTH

The hands of God work mysteriously, but always with skill and love.

MY FAITHFUL LOVE FOREVER

*I will betroth you to me forever. . .in faithfulness,
and you will acknowledge the LORD.*

HOSEA 2:19–20

FROM THE FATHER'S HEART

My child, I courted you long before you loved Me. I loved you when you were unlovable. And even when you turned away from Me for a season and ran after other lovers, I chased you with My love. I waited for you, like a father for his prodigal son. You can never run too far away. I'm not about to lose your love, My bride. I will search for you to the ends of the earth and bring you back. I love you that much. I keep my covenants. I remain your faithful love forever.

A GRATEFUL RESPONSE

You are my faithful love, forever pledging compassion and faithfulness to me. Even when I've turned away, You have not divorced me, Lord. You looked deep inside my heart and loved me not for what I was, but for what I could be in You. I love You, Lord. How could I ever leave You?

SIMPLE TRUTH

Jesus—always love, always joy, always peace.

CONTINUITY

Your faithfulness continues through all generations;
you established the earth,
and it endures.

PSALM 119:90

FROM THE FATHER'S HEART

My child, nothing ever changes about My character. I am the same, day after day. But you are like a chameleon, changing "colors" and attitudes as often as the weather. I understand, My child. I know you are as dust. But let My continuity be an example of faithfulness to you. Daily, come, sit and talk with Me. The more we get together, the more stable your life will become. My ultimate goal is to make you like Me so others will see My reflection in your life.

A GRATEFUL RESPONSE

My life is so seasonal, Lord. In springtime, I bask in Your showers of blessing; in summer, I rest in Your grace; in fall, I'm that leaf hanging on for dear life; and in winter, I'm as cold as icy glaze. But with Your continuity, forever the same, it's always springtime in my heart.

SIMPLE TRUTH

Jesus gives a standing invitation: He requests the
honor of your presence—daily.

ALL IN ALL

Here there is no Greek or Jew,
circumcised or uncircumcised, barbarian, Scythian,
slave or free, but Christ is all, and is in all.

COLOSSIANS 3:11

FROM THE FATHER'S HEART

My child, I see the prejudice in people's lives—even in My children—and it disturbs Me greatly.

Have I not created all equally? Are not all human hearts moldable? Did I not die for every person on the face of this earth? Let your love be an example to others, My child. Will you let Me make your heart a channel of open blessing that accepts all regardless of race, color, or creed? Will you tell them I love all people the same?

A GRATEFUL RESPONSE

Jesus, You cross every barrier of race, creed, or color. You're a gentle lullaby to the babe in arms and a loving father to every child. To the lonely, You're a companion, and to the hurting, You are a comforter. To the parent, You're a guide, and to the aged, an encourager. And to me? Lord, You're all those things and more. You're my all in all.

SIMPLE TRUTH

Jesus is all in all—to all.

GLORIOUS LORD

But there the glorious LORD will be unto us
a place of broad rivers and streams.

Isaiah 33:21 KJV

From the Father's Heart

My child, in this world your streets may seem narrow and confining. Troubles come and troubles go and leave you without strength to forge ahead. But I am your glorious Lord and will fill you with might and strength. I will make you like a spring of living water—so you can taste a fraction of the joy waiting for you in heaven someday. There, streams will flow freely; sickness will not reign, and suffering will end. I will be there waiting for you to step across.

A Grateful Response

Lord, Your kingdom is not of this world; Your thoughts are not like ours. You are the glorious Lord, magnificent in nature, excellent and infinite. One day this narrow road we travel will broaden into eternal rivers and streets of gold, and You will receive the glory You so richly deserve.

Simple Truth

Our times are in His hands—even the times we don't understand.

INFALLIBILITY

All your words are true;
all your righteous laws are eternal.

PSALM 119:160

FROM THE FATHER'S HEART

My child, you can never add or subtract anything from My words. They are infallible, as am I. Others may try to change the rules in midstream, reinventing codes and creeds that fit their lifestyles and pleasures. But My Word and My principles still stand. Test them, My child. See if I will not pour out a blessing upon you and the ones for whom you pray. Trust My decisions and My infallible character. You will see one day how the puzzle of your life fits together.

A GRATEFUL RESPONSE

You are the only One who ever lived that has infallibility. Human error abounds, but You are the perfect rose, the spotless lamb, the purest gold. Though You make allowance for my errors, You never make mistakes.

SIMPLE TRUTH

Our perfectionism will drive us to failure, but our
dependency will lead us to God.

INDESCRIBABLE GIFT

*Thanks be to God
for his indescribable gift!*

2 CORINTHIANS 9:15

FROM THE FATHER'S HEART

My child, the next time you are feeling unimportant or slighted, remember again My indescribable gift to you—the gift of Myself. To the common observer, My life on earth had a humble beginning and a tragic ending. But the trained eye will recognize heaven's love gift as the One to all the world. I exclude no one. Those who reject the gift choose their own fate. Take the indescribable gift of My presence—and offer it to those I send your way. It will change their lives forever.

A GRATEFUL RESPONSE

Of all the gifts I've ever received, none compares to You, Lord. You are the indescribable gift, packaged with love and sent with heaven's blessing. Thank You for the wonderful gift of Yourself—the gift that keeps on giving and giving.

SIMPLE TRUTH

*One heart to give in simple faith, one testimony true,
one gift, one song, one life, one heart—I give them,
Lord, to You.*

LORD GOD ALMIGHTY

Day and night they never stop saying:
"Holy, holy, holy is the Lord God Almighty, who was,
and is, and is to come."

REVELATION 4:8

FROM THE FATHER'S HEART

My child, praises are beautiful to My ears. The angels worship Me daily. Their voices fill the halls of heaven with sweet melody. But what really delights Me is to hear the music of your life, My child. I long to hear your praises. Has anything silenced your voice? Let Me remove it and turn the minor notes into a major symphony. I am the Lord God Almighty, the One who first gave you a song. Listen carefully. Do you hear the music stirring again?

A GRATEFUL RESPONSE

Lord, at times Your name brings ambivalent feelings. Strength, majesty, omniscience, holiness—all stir up a reverent fear. And yet Your goodness, faithfulness, and love draw me closer to You as a personal God. How I long to bow before You like the angels, and in Your presence sing "Holy, Holy, Holy" day and night. In all ways, You are the Lord God Almighty—of the past, present, and future.

SIMPLE TRUTH

Even the deaf ear can hear the music if it is in touch
with the great musician.

GENTLENESS

By the meekness and gentleness of Christ,
I appeal to you.

2 Corinthians 10:1

From the Father's Heart

My child, is My gentleness such a difficult character trait to mirror? Perhaps it is because you confuse it with weakness. I only reflect My Father's personality. If the awesome God of the universe, who has all power and all might, could still care about the fall of one sparrow or hug a child to His heart with the tender love of a mother, can you not believe gentleness is a virtue? Let Me fill you with My gentleness. It's impossible on your own.

A Grateful Response

The gentleness of Jesus is not just for babes, but for every one of God's children. Lord, You treat each one of us as a fragile flower, a delicate blossom to be handled with care. Thank You for Your gentle and personal attention.

Simple Truth

Jesus is God's personal hug to us.

MESSENGER

*"See, I will send my messenger,
who will prepare the way before me."*

Malachi 3:1

From the Father's Heart

My child, no matter how many messengers I send, many will still reject Me. I even came in person, a flesh and blood divine messenger—the Son of God. Yet My own people turned away. My child, I still want to draw everyone to Myself—and into My Father's kingdom. I long to fill hearts with peace, joy, and eternal life. I'm so glad you listened to My message.

A Grateful Response

Throughout Scripture You made Yourself known—through angels to guard and guide, to strengthen and save, to encourage and sustain; through prophets to warn and correct and draw to Yourself. You are God's own messenger, a heaven-sent gift to earth, making the ways of God known.

Simple Truth

*To the heart that seeks His own, God will make the
path straight and His ways known.*

EVERLASTING ARMS

The eternal God is your refuge,
and underneath are the everlasting arms.

DEUTERONOMY 33:27

FROM THE FATHER'S HEART

My child, do you fear stepping out in faith? Are you like that baby eagle, trembling before you try out your wings? Are you looking down at the ground or up at the sky? Remember, at the moment you exercise your faith wings, I am there to catch you if you fall. Underneath the thin air you will find a cushion awaiting your landing. My everlasting arms will be your pillow.

A GRATEFUL RESPONSE

When I'm afraid or hurting, I run to You to find refuge. Halfway there, You meet me, Lord, with arms open wide. Tenderly, You scoop me up, and there, in Your everlasting arms, I rest until the fear and pain are gone. You're such a comfort, Lord.

SIMPLE TRUTH

Faith gives wings to our dreams.

HOLINESS

Worship the Lord
in the splendor of his holiness.

PSALM 29:2

FROM THE FATHER'S HEART

My child, can holiness fellowship with unholiness? No, but by My death and resurrection, through My shed blood and sacrifice for you, and because of your choice to enter My presence through a life of faith, I have declared you holy, too, My child. I have draped My righteous nature over you, so that when you come into My presence, you are clean. Once you are My child, you are My child forever.

A GRATEFUL RESPONSE

Standing in Your presence brings such a sense of awe, Lord. Looking at Your holiness is like looking at my life under a microscope, revealing every flaw and imperfection in exaggerated detail. You are perfect, Lord. I praise You for Your holiness.

SIMPLE TRUTH

Begin the day with praise. End the day with thanksgiving.

THE OIL OF GLADNESS

To bestow on them a crown of beauty instead of ashes,
the oil of gladness instead of mourning. . . .

ISAIAH 61:3

FROM THE FATHER'S HEART

My child, My Father anointed Me for such a time as this. I came to bring beauty from ashes, to turn mourning to song, and to grant freedom from captivity. Give Me all of your ashes, all your hurts. That's why I'm here. Where sin has ravaged your life, I will restore. Where despair has left you wounded, I will heal. I am the oil of gladness. I have abundant joy for you, My child!

A GRATEFUL RESPONSE

You visited my heart where only bitter sadness lived. Where years of pain had stripped away its immunity, You came as the oil of gladness, offering healing and restoration. You soothed the weary places and brought new hope to me. I find my joy in You, Lord.

SIMPLE TRUTH

God never wastes the scraps of our lives, but fashions
something beautiful out of each piece.

LIGHT OF ISRAEL

The Light of Israel
will become a fire.

ISAIAH 10:17

FROM THE FATHER'S HEART

My child, I am the Light of Israel, but I am also the Light of the world. The same light that ushers in new understanding into a world of darkness will spark a flame that consumes every wicked intention under the sun. Don't run from the Light, My child. When I light the way for you to move another step ahead, rejoice. But when I see you following after wrong influences, remember that My love is also a flame of correction, drawing you back, burning away the chaff. Receive My purifying fire with joy, as well. It means I still love you.

A GRATEFUL RESPONSE

Just like You led Your chosen people, Israel, out of the darkness into the light, You shine brightly in my world today. The rays of Your brightness warm every corner of my life. You are the Light of Israel, but You are my light, too.

SIMPLE TRUTH

It only takes a spark to make a flame.

DISCRETION

"Do not give dogs what is sacred;
do not throw your pearls to pigs."

MATTHEW 7:6

FROM THE FATHER'S HEART

My child, I have chosen earthen vessels like you to hold My most valuable jewels because My light shines best in ordinary people. Others, full of themselves or with the cares of this world, have stuffed their jars so full, there is no room left for Me. Use My discretion wisely, My child. Sacred things are not to be trampled, but preserved. Share My treasures wisely. Don't hoard them, but give them to faithful disciples who appreciate the value.

A GRATEFUL RESPONSE

Not everyone can appreciate the "diviner" things of life, Lord. You were careful to give Your jewels to those who would value their worth. I appreciate Your discretion, Lord. And I thank You for entrusting me with Your valuables.

SIMPLE TRUTH

Even in the darkness there are treasures of light.

PLANTER

*They will be called oaks of righteousness,
a planting of the LORD for the display of his splendor.*

ISAIAH 61:3

FROM THE FATHER'S HEART

My child, do you sometimes feel like a tiny acorn surrounded by huge oak trees? I hear your sighs. I know how badly you want to grow, yet there are times you may see no progress at all. Trust Me. I am the planter. It takes years to grow a sturdy oak. Don't be impatient. Just because you can't see the branches doesn't mean My power is not at work in you. Your labor is not in vain. In time, you, too, will become an oak that offers shade and blessing to many.

A GRATEFUL RESPONSE

At times I've wished to be a strong, sturdy oak, or maybe a pine whose green branches grace the forest all year. Yet sometimes I feel like I'll always be a twig. You decide what I'll be, according to Your divine plan. I'll bloom, Lord, wherever I'm planted.

SIMPLE TRUTH
He is the planter; we are the seed.

Day 304

INVISIBLE GOD

He is the image of the invisible God.

COLOSSIANS 1:15

FROM THE FATHER'S HEART

My child, others scoff at your declarations that I am real, living in you and all around you. But not everyone can see Me. I am the invisible God, and I am spirit discerned. When Moses saw My glory, others could not even look at his face. But he looked with eyes of faith. The heart can see what the physical eye cannot. If you search for Me, you'll find Me.

A GRATEFUL RESPONSE

You are like the wind whispering through the pines, like a ripple by the water's edge. I cannot see You, but I feel Your awesome presence all around me. You are the invisible God, and I can only visualize You with eyes of faith. But You are there, Lord, always there.

SIMPLE TRUTH

When we look for God, we'll find Him, right where He's always been.

CAPABILITY

"For nothing is impossible with God."

LUKE 1:37

FROM THE FATHER'S HEART

My child, I love the word impossible! Don't you? I know you believe I can do anything. Yes, I have the capability to do anything. But you're unsure if I will do what you ask. Ask anything in My name, and I will do anything according to My will. My child, do you know what I'm really after? Your total, sold-out heart. If you can ask Me anything your heart desires, but tell Me however I answer is really okay with you, I know I truly have your heart.

A GRATEFUL RESPONSE

Who can limit Your power? Who are we to question what You can or cannot do? You, who hold the keys to heaven and hell, You, who spoke the world into existence; You are not confined by walls or fences. Thank You for Your capability, Lord. There is nothing too hard for You to do. Lord, I want to trust You even more.

SIMPLE TRUTH

There is no miracle out of God's reach.

Day 306

PERMANENT PRIEST

*But because Jesus lives forever,
he has a permanent priesthood.*

HEBREWS 7:24

FROM THE FATHER'S HEART

My child, My high priests served their purpose well. I commissioned each one to offer sacrifices for My people of old, to be the intercessor between God and man. But they are gone, and the sacrifices have died with them. Know that I am your high priest forever. I have a permanent priesthood that offers complete salvation, unconditional love, and total forgiveness. I offered Myself as the ultimate, perfect sacrifice for you. I initiated the New Covenant—and you accepted. I'm so glad you did.

A GRATEFUL RESPONSE

Just like passing shadows, Your priests have come and gone. But You, Lord, are the permanent priest. Because You intercede for me, I can proceed to God. Because of You, the Father hears my name often and welcomes me to His throne.

SIMPLE TRUTH
When you call on God, there's no long distance charge.

TOWER

The name of the LORD is a strong tower;
the righteous run to it and are safe.

PROVERBS 18:10

FROM THE FATHER'S HEART

My child, when terror rises up like an erupting volcano, stop, drop, and pray. Cry out to Me, and in those precious moments, you will feel a surge of courage as you've never known. Call My name, and you'll sense an invisible tower looming out of nowhere. Run to it. I'll be waiting there for you with open arms.

A GRATEFUL RESPONSE

I cry, "Father," and a thousand currents of lightning carry Your name to the highest heavens. Farther than the eye can see or the ear can hear, You are waiting to rescue me. You are my tower, a place of safety and refuge daily.

SIMPLE TRUTH

We need not fear, for with every step, and in every place, God is near.

BEAUTY

One thing I ask of the LORD. . .
to gaze upon the beauty of the LORD
and to seek him in his temple.

PSALM 27:4

FROM THE FATHER'S HEART

My child, My beauty is for you to enjoy. Everything I've created, I've made for you. Look around. There's beauty in the earth and skies, in every field and flower, in every creature that walks on earth. And My beauty is in you, Child. You don't see it? Maybe it's because you're looking in the wrong mirror again. You are beautiful to Me.

A GRATEFUL RESPONSE

When I think about the beauty of Your creation, who am I, Lord, that You consider me? Yet as magnificent as Your works are, there is no comparison to Your own beauty. My one desire is to be a God-seeker, not a people-pleaser, and that I could live in Your home and worship You forever. Lord, You are so beautiful.

SIMPLE TRUTH

Beauty is in the eyes of the believer.

PURSUER

> *"Why do you pursue me
> as God does?"*
>
> JOB 19:22

FROM THE FATHER'S HEART

My child, I will never smother you. I always give you space to make your own decisions. But I have invested much into your life, and I intend to make sure that investment is safe. I am your pursuer, but not in the same way as others. They chase you with thoughtless opinions and prideful words, always trying to persuade you to accept their point of view. I am your "hound of heaven," and I will track you down wherever you go, just to keep you close to Me. May you always feel My breath upon your spirit.

A GRATEFUL RESPONSE

Like one searching out his lost love, You are my pursuer. You chase after me with blessings too numerous to count. You do not pursue me to punish me, but to draw me closer to Your love. How could I ever leave the security of Your arms?

SIMPLE TRUTH

You will never pursue a greater love than Jesus.

LANDOWNER

"For the kingdom of heaven is like a landowner
who went out early in the morning
to hire men to work in his vineyard."

MATTHEW 20:1

FROM THE FATHER'S HEART

My child, I not only own the cattle on a thousand hills, but I own the hills where the cattle graze. As landowner, I own everything. Whomever I choose to work in My kingdom is My decision. And, speaking of workers, I have something special for you to do, designed exactly for your abilities and gifts. At times, I may even stretch your limits so you'll know I did the work through you. Don't envy others' opportunities or rewards. You will receive a wonderful "well done" in heaven when you follow Me faithfully. Trust Me.

A GRATEFUL RESPONSE

You are the landowner, calling out workers for Your kingdom. It's not up to me to judge Your business practices, for You have been more than fair to me. I deserve no pay for working but instead owe You my life. I am the least of Your kingdom. Because of You, I'm never unemployed.

SIMPLE TRUTH

If we all received what we deserved, we would all be paupers.

KNOWLEDGE

*"Can anyone teach knowledge to God,
since he judges even the highest?"*

JOB 21:22

FROM THE FATHER'S HEART

My child, pride is a dangerous thing. Be careful, lest the knowledge you acquire puff you up and make you obnoxious to others. The one who gives ready answers without thinking is like a cloud that brings no rain. I am knowledge itself, and though learning from others is beneficial, I am your ultimate source of information. Check out My words in Scripture. There, you'll find everything you need for holy and righteous living. Knowledge without love is useless.

A GRATEFUL RESPONSE

Those who tried to confuse and correct You were silenced by Your knowledge, Lord. Who can argue with the God of the universe? Who would dare to correct the God Most High? Yet at times, even I have questioned You, Lord. Your knowledge is too great for me to begin to understand.

SIMPLE TRUTH

Better to have a big heart than a big head.

RANSOM

"Just as the Son of Man did not come to be served,
but to serve, and to give his life as a ransom for many."

MATTHEW 20:28

FROM THE FATHER'S HEART

My child, all the wealth in the world could not supply hope and eternal life for you. No bank could afford the loan it would take to pay for your sins. When My enemy threatened your life and your destiny, I intervened. I became the ransom, the ultimate payment, so you could live free forever. I put all your enemies out of business forever. So remember, if they come around again, bluffing, just send them to Me. I'll take care of them.

A GRATEFUL RESPONSE

When I was kidnapped by sin, with no possibility of freedom, You laid down Your life for me. You were the ransom, the price paid to set me free. You took my death and my pain. You exchanged Your life for mine. I am no longer a prisoner, Lord—all because of You.

SIMPLE TRUTH

In God's family, He allows no kidnapping.

GOD OF THE LIVING

*"He is not the God of the dead
but of the living."*

MATTHEW 22:32

FROM THE FATHER'S HEART

My child, all of the "great" people you've read about in the past, those who had large followings, have one thing in common: They're all dead. Not one of them can claim to be God of the living as I do. When My followers die, it is only a step across heaven's threshold, like going from one room in your house to another. Only this house will be like none you have ever seen. I'm excited just thinking about all I've planned for you.

A GRATEFUL RESPONSE

Lord, I'm waiting for the day the clouds will part, opening up the heavens to announce Your second arrival. Whether from the grave, or from my home, I'll listen for Your "Arise!" You are God of the living, Lord. And I'll be part of the greater resurrection. What an exciting event!

SIMPLE TRUTH

*You will not find Jesus in a garden where a soldier
stands guard. Instead, you will find Jesus waiting at
the entrance of your heart.*

AGGRESSIVENESS

He struck down many nations
and killed mighty kings.

PSALM 135:10

FROM THE FATHER'S HEART

My child, there is a time to defend and a time to play the offensive. I am a holy God, and I hold nations accountable for what they do with their knowledge, and with the claims they make about Christianity. I never overlook injustice, nor do I reward wickedness. Aggressiveness is part of My nature, just like gentleness. When you hear of wars and rumors of wars, My child, don't be afraid. I'm still in control. I'm still on My throne, and I take care of My own.

A GRATEFUL RESPONSE

Lord, Your other side is like a storming force of nature. As a tornado ruthlessly creates its own path, Your aggressiveness doles out fairness and just reward to those who refuse to accept You. Each person has a choice to make. I choose You as Lord of my life.

SIMPLE TRUTH

Character is what is left when adversity steals your
dream. It's the force that drives you forward when
others leave the team.

REWARDER

*Because anyone who comes to him must believe that he exists
and that he rewards those who earnestly seek him.*

HEBREWS 11:6

FROM THE FATHER'S HEART

My child, do you know how much I enjoy rewarding My
children? I love when you go on treasure hunts in My Word.
I've hidden so many special treats there, just for your eyes.
They will bless your socks off! I am the rewarder of those
who diligently seek Me with their whole hearts. I've never
yet turned away one who sincerely came looking for Me,
and who really believed who I was. And I never will. Some
rewards are for now; others are waiting for you in heaven.
Your faith, My child, is what pleases Me.

A GRATEFUL RESPONSE

Lord, You do not play hide and seek with Your children.
You're the rewarder, always waiting at the end of my search,
like the pot of gold at the end of the rainbow. Lord, the reward of Your applause, Your familiar "well done," is all that
really matters.

SIMPLE TRUTH

Each journey with God is an adventure of faith.

DEFENSE

But the LORD is my defence;
and my God is the rock of my refuge.

PSALM 94:22 KJV

FROM THE FATHER'S HEART

My child, do I need to open your eyes as I did to My servant long ago? In the heat of battling your habits and temptations, or when circumstances try your patience and faith, remember I am your defense. My angels do hand-to-hand combat at My command. You may not see them, but they surround you, day in and day out. Open your eyes of faith. The battle is Mine.

A GRATEFUL RESPONSE

Like a veteran returning home from foreign wars, I see the scars of battle, those incurred when I fought apart from Your strength. But when I depend on You alone to man the front line for me, I'm a victor every time. Lord, thank You for being my defense. I'm glad You're on my side.

SIMPLE TRUTH

Like a shining star, He lights our path, even in
the dark.

Day 317

TRUSTWORTHINESS

The angel said to me,
"These words are trustworthy and true."

REVELATION 22:6

FROM THE FATHER'S HEART

My child, have you read My account lately of heaven and of life's final events? Exciting, isn't it? You don't understand it all? You don't have to. Sounds too beautiful to be true? Golden streets, crystal rivers, tree of life with fruit for healing—trust Me, My child. These pictures can't begin to describe the beauty of heaven. My name and My words are the same. I am Trustworthiness—and everything I have said in My Word I will do.

A GRATEFUL RESPONSE

From Your very first command, "Let there be light," to the last "Amen" announcing Your second coming, You have trustworthiness. Not a single word will pass away, not a word of truth will be lost, because Your words never return void. How faithful You have been in my life! I trust You, Lord.

SIMPLE TRUTH

God has prepared a place where every dream can find fulfillment, and every hope can find a home.

ILLUMINATION

He had great authority,
and the earth was illuminated
by his splendor.

REVELATION 18:1

FROM THE FATHER'S HEART

My child, remember that bad things do happen to good people. You live in a fallen world. But in your darkness, I will provide light. Brighter than any angel's splendor or shining sun, I am the light. As your illumination, I will push back the dark corners of your life until you can see clearly again. I will never leave you without hope—or light.

A GRATEFUL RESPONSE

Soon after the twilight hours are gone, as light seems to fade sadly into darkness, there You are, Lord, shining as a lighthouse to guide me through the night. And soon my darkness is past, for You, my illumination, have appeared. Thank You for Your presence, Lord.

SIMPLE TRUTH

Jesus is the light of the world. We are His matches.

Day 319

FULFILLMENT OF PROPHECY

And he made known to us the mystery of his will. . .
which he purposed in Christ,
to be put into effect when the times will have
reached their fulfillment.

EPHESIANS 1:9–10

FROM THE FATHER'S HEART

My child, if you want to know where history fits into My plans, go back and read My prophecies. Every one of them concerning the coming of Messiah has been fulfilled. I am the fulfillment of prophecy, the long-awaited promise from the beginning. And stay tuned for more. You're seeing fulfillment of prophecy every day. Don't be frightened. You're a part of My glorious history unfolding. And I'm Lord of the future, too.

A GRATEFUL RESPONSE

Reading the newspaper is like watching history unfold before my eyes. Lord, You are the fulfillment of prophecy. From the beginning of time, God ordained Your coming. Men foretold it, but God accomplished it. The dark clouds are beginning to clear. Come soon, Lord Jesus.

SIMPLE TRUTH

There is no one like Jesus who is more worthy of honor and praise.

VALIDITY

"There is another who testifies in my favor,
and I know that his testimony about me is valid."

JOHN 5:32

FROM THE FATHER'S HEART

My child, the law required two witnesses to verify the truth
about someone's character and testimony. Though I had
many witnesses, I needed none: I had validity in My works
and My Father's words. Yet so many refused to believe in
Me. They still do. Just like My faithful servant John the
Baptist who testified about My coming and prepared the
way, will you, too, help prepare a place in someone's heart
for Me? Do it today, Child. Time is short.

A GRATEFUL RESPONSE

Just like the instruments directing a ship to its harbor, Your
life and testimony have validity. Your personal witnesses—
the bruised, the broken, the dead made alive, the sick who
were healed—all believed You, Lord. But more than that,
the Father Himself verified who You were. I'll be Your witness, too, Lord.

SIMPLE TRUTH

It's not where you've been or what you've done, but
whose you are that matters most.

DESTROYER

*The reason the Son of God appeared was
to destroy the devil's work.*

1 JOHN 3:8

FROM THE FATHER'S HEART

My child, don't believe when others say I am out to get you.
I did not come to destroy the world, but to save it. Men and
women choose to destroy themselves because they reject Me
and My love. You have only one real enemy, and he is real,
but full of hot air. He will come to you trying to deceive you
with lies about Me and about you. Resist him in My name.
I came to destroy his efforts. I won, Child. He cannot harm
you. I'm greater than your enemy.

A GRATEFUL RESPONSE

The earth and all that's in it are at Your mercy, Lord. Though
You could destroy every living thing with one swift blow,
You came to crush the devil, not us. You are the destroyer of
evil. You are the One who has already won.

SIMPLE TRUTH

*When you're on God's side, Satan is all roar and no
bite.*

THE FAITHFUL WITNESS

Grace and peace to you. . .and from Jesus Christ, who is the faithful witness.

REVELATION 1:4–5

FROM THE FATHER'S HEART

My child, I hold the key to what the Father is like. I am the only One who knows. I and My Father are the same. When you see Me, you see Him. So when you need to know truth, come to Me. I am the faithful witness. I've existed before the world ever did, so I'm witness to what has taken place throughout the halls of history. Trust Me, Child. I never lie or deceive.

A GRATEFUL RESPONSE

Lord, Your words and deeds spread like a forest fire, burning and refining those in Your path. You are the faithful witness, an accurate testimony to the real nature of God. You not only testify to the truth, but You are the Truth.

SIMPLE TRUTH

To know Him, to love Him, to make His ways known—is there any goal more worthy to pursue as our own?

THOUGHTFULNESS

How precious to me are your thoughts, O God!
How vast is the sum of them!

PSALM 139:17

FROM THE FATHER'S HEART

My child, I'm thrilled to see you today. I always am. You were on My mind long before your birth, and every day I'm thinking up new ways to bless you and use you to bless others. If you tried to count My thoughts, you'd tire before the day ended. They are as numerous as the grains of sand on the beach. How do I really feel about you? Precious is your middle name. I hope you'll always feel the same about Me.

A GRATEFUL RESPONSE

You never forget my birthday, Lord. You're always thinking of me. Before my eyes can greet the early morning's sun, before my ears can hear the robin's first song, You're already waiting to greet me with loving anticipation. Lord, thank You for Your thoughtfulness to me.

SIMPLE TRUTH

There's not a single day but what God thinks of us
some way.

HOPE OF GLORY

*To them God has chosen to make known among the Gentiles
the glorious riches of this mystery,
which is Christ in you, the hope of glory.*

COLOSSIANS 1:27

FROM THE FATHER'S HEART

My child, if you never had any tunnels to go through, and if you never experienced despair, why would you need hope? I have a purpose in everything, even suffering. Sometimes that purpose is to show you that I am your only hope of glory. I'm the only One who knows the intricate mysteries of life. And I choose to pour out those riches to you, My child, because you are in Christ. In darkness or in light, I will always be that hope for you.

A GRATEFUL RESPONSE

When hope is only a dot on the horizon, You flood my life with showers of encouragement. My hope is in You, Lord: You are my destination; You are my consolation; You are my celebration. You are Christ in me, my hope of glory.

SIMPLE TRUTH

Hope is a paint drop of color in an ordinary day.

WRITER

*"I will put my law
in their minds and write it
on their hearts."*

JEREMIAH 31:33

FROM THE FATHER'S HEART

My child, you're not judged by the law anymore. You now live by My grace. I am the writer of every inspired word in My Holy Scriptures. But I have penned My message in your heart through the power of the Holy Spirit. I now live in you. Each time you meditate on My Word, act out My love to others, and respond in obedience, you are allowing Me to write My signature on your heart and life. Some people will look to you as their Bible. Be faithful to share My words.

A GRATEFUL RESPONSE

Lord, Your work has made the best-seller list for hundreds of years. You are the author and writer of the most powerful book ever known. But more than that, You've written Your words permanently in my heart. And nothing can erase what You have written with Your own hands.

SIMPLE TRUTH

God is not looking for best-sellers, only faithful witnesses.

ORIGINALITY

For you created my inmost being;
you knit me together
in my mother's womb.

PSALM 139:13

FROM THE FATHER'S HEART

My child, your frame was not a haphazard creation. I didn't use the same mold to make cookie-cutter shapes and sizes for My children. Each one is original. No composites of DNA can ever completely duplicate your heart, soul, and spirit as I created you. I took great delight in watching each tiny finger and toe being formed in the womb. And when your tiny heart first beat within your mother, all the angels could hear Me rejoice. I make no mistakes. You're special to Me, My child.

A GRATEFUL RESPONSE

You design each of us with intricate and delicate care, just like a tiny snowflake. There are no two the same, for You specialize in originality. Lord, You created me as one of a kind, with my own unique, designer genes. You're the best, Lord.

SIMPLE TRUTH

After God breathed life into you, He destroyed the mold.

CARETAKER

You care for the land and water it; you enrich it abundantly.
You crown the year with your bounty,
and your carts overflow with abundance.

PSALM 65:9, 11

FROM THE FATHER'S HEART

My child, I take good care of what is Mine. I help each sparrow find a nest, a home for its young. I provide water for the thirsty, panting deer and food for the beasts of every forest. But I especially love supplying your needs. You are more valuable than all of My creation put together. I am your caretaker, Child. Will you take care of what I have given you, too?

A GRATEFUL RESPONSE

Lord, You send a harvest of blessing our way to crown the season with Thanksgiving Day. You are caretaker of Your world, and You have provided abundantly everything I need and more for joy and contentment. How can I thank You, Lord? Bless You for Your faithfulness, Lord.

SIMPLE TRUTH

Thanksgiving is "thanksliving."

FLAME

Their Holy One [will become] a flame;
in a single day it will burn
and consume his thorns and his briers.

ISAIAH 10:17

FROM THE FATHER'S HEART

My child, we've sat together by the "fire" many times—some days enjoying the warmth of a physical fireplace, other times holding hands at the bedside of a dying loved one. I am also a flame, a fire to light the hearts of people who are cold and distant, and a destroyer of accumulated trash in the rooms of My children's hearts. But whatever I do, I always act in love. Never forget that, My child. You'll be pleased with the end result if you'll let Me be God.

A GRATEFUL RESPONSE

You are an eternal flame, Lord. While Your wrath leaves only ashes in the path of Your enemies, Your flame burns brightly in my heart, warming up the coldness and apathy I've allowed to grow. Lord, You are the flame of my life.

SIMPLE TRUTH

If God isn't the consuming fire in your heart, maybe
you need to put out some other flames.

OMNIPRESENCE

Where can I go from your Spirit?
Where can I flee from your presence?

PSALM 139:7

FROM THE FATHER'S HEART

My child, no matter how far you run from Me, you cannot escape My love or My presence. My eyes see your every action; My heart feels your every pain; My Spirit lives within you and travels wherever you go. My love will chase you down, but I will never force you to return. As long as you live, I will continue to call your name until you let Me back in as the keeper and ruler of your heart. I'm omnipresent, Child. I'm with you always.

A GRATEFUL RESPONSE

At times I may be alone, but I'm never lonely. Your Spirit surrounds me wherever I go. In the garden's sweet fragrance, on the storm-tossed sea, in the highest heavens, and beneath the deepest ocean, You are there, Lord. Your presence is inescapable. Lord, why would I ever leave the joy of Your presence? You are omnipresent—always near. Thanks for being there, Lord.

SIMPLE TRUTH

Love keeps us close to the heart of God.

INSPIRATION

*For prophecy never had its origin in the will of man,
but men spoke from God as they were carried
along by the Holy Spirit.*

2 PETER 1:21

FROM THE FATHER'S HEART

My child, no one ever speaks the truth about Me without My Father revealing that truth to them. They are not capable of knowing Me apart from My Spirit, which draws them to Me and indwells them with My presence. I inspired the prophets to speak only the words I told them. A true prophet's words came to pass because My Spirit breathed them into the heart. As I was with them, let Me be your inspiration. Think and write thoughts that only glorify Me.

A GRATEFUL RESPONSE

Just as You inspired writers and prophets long ago, You are my inspiration today. You breathe into me the fresh breezes of Your love and goodness. Each day brings a new opportunity to catch Your blessings. And Lord, there are so many!

SIMPLE TRUTH

*Prayer is a gift we can give, when words are too deep
to be spoken.*

GUARDIAN

Set a guard over my mouth, O LORD;
keep watch over the door of my lips.

PSALM 141:3

FROM THE FATHER'S HEART

My child, learn to pick your battles. Is it really worth losing a friend or loved one over things? Can you fix others' problems by playing God in their lives? Can you retrieve a poison dart once it hits the target? Let Me be your guardian. I'll station My angels like an armed guard around your mouth and your heart. And My Spirit will seal your lips before you make a costly mistake. It will help if you hide My words in your heart. That's where ugly thoughts are born.

A GRATEFUL RESPONSE

Lord, my lips can either be like a fresh spring or a bitter stream. You are my guardian, keeping watch not just over the door of my lips, but through the window of my heart. With my words, with my heart, with my life, Lord, I want to praise You.

SIMPLE TRUTH

Loving words are like buried treasure. When we find
them and give them away, they bring great delight.

RECONCILIATION

Not only is this so,
but we also rejoice in God through our Lord Jesus Christ,
through whom we have now received reconciliation.

ROMANS 5:11

FROM THE FATHER'S HEART

My child, have you ever tried to step into the middle of an argument and negotiate an impossible situation? Because of your own sin nature, you literally stood on one side of the world and God on the other. But the good news is that My death brought you together. I stepped in the middle and brought a Holy God into the same room with you—who even now sits at the same table of fellowship. I provided reconciliation—and forgiveness. Your sins, which were numerous, are now as far away as the east from the west. Aren't you glad you're a child of God?

A GRATEFUL RESPONSE

Lord, You are my reconciliation, my only access to the Father. Like darkness joining the light, spring welcoming winter, the lion befriending the lamb, You have opened the door to the Father's own heart. Your life was the bridge that took me there. Thank You, Jesus.

SIMPLE TRUTH

God is as near to you as the prayer of your heart.

TENACITY

*By oppression and judgment
he was taken away.
And who can speak of his descendants?*

ISAIAH 53:8

FROM THE FATHER'S HEART

My child, if I had quit the night of My greatest temptation in the Garden of Gethsemane and refused to do My Father's will, where do you think you would be? I loved you too much to act selfishly. The next time you are tempted to do your own thing or to shirk the tasks I've given you, remember My tenacity. Hold on to your faith—and to My hand. You won't be sorry.

A GRATEFUL RESPONSE

Lord, You won no popularity contests. No one voted You "Most Likely to Succeed." While You were here on earth, You were despised and forsaken. Yet, You held on, like the last rose before winter. And what a garden of "flowers" You produced! Thank You for Your tenacity, Lord.

SIMPLE TRUTH

Determination is the ability to channel yesterday's lessons into tomorrow's dreams.

GUILT OFFERING

And though the LORD makes his life a guilt offering,
he will see his offspring and prolong his days.

ISAIAH 53:10

FROM THE FATHER'S HEART

My child, if there had been another way to cover your guilt, My Father would have chosen it. But it took My life, a willing sacrifice, to pay for the sins of all My children. No longer would the high priest lead the scapegoat outside the tent to appease a Holy God. Instead, I became the once and for all guilt offering. I was led "out of the camp," to the outskirts of Jerusalem where I was crucified for you. Just for the love of you, My child.

A GRATEFUL RESPONSE

You were the scapegoat for my failures, Lord, the guilt offering sacrificed on my behalf. You, who knew no guilt; You, who were never tainted by sin; You, whose very name spelled purity and holiness—You gave Your very life for me. Can I ever thank You enough?

SIMPLE TRUTH

We're a special part of God's own heart.

DAYSPRING

Through the tender mercy of our God;
whereby the dayspring from on high hath visited us.

LUKE 1:78 KJV

FROM THE FATHER'S HEART

My child, as surely as the sun descends, it will rise again the next day. I am your eternal dayspring, the rising sun of every morning. I am the One who shone on the world with My birth, and I am the One who shines in your darkness. I visited the world with My salvation. But I live in your heart daily, making you more and more like Myself—so you can shine for My glory.

A GRATEFUL RESPONSE

I face the midnight hours, tossing from the day's weariness. Worries stand in line, begging for attention. But all night, behind the scenes, You are intercepting my thoughts. When the dawn greets me, I feel refreshed. You, the dayspring, have renewed my heart.

SIMPLE TRUTH
Our light shines best when the Son is in full view.

TRANQUILITY

Without warning, a furious storm came up on the lake,
so that the waves swept over the boat.
But Jesus was sleeping.

MATTHEW 8:24

FROM THE FATHER'S HEART

My child, you need reminders often that I am Lord of your rocking boat. You may think I'm asleep, but I never slumber or sleep. My eyes are always riveted on the world—and on My children's lives. But there is more at stake than your small world can acknowledge. Rest, Child. Just rest in Me. Others need your peace, not your frantic worry. Let Me be your tranquility.

A GRATEFUL RESPONSE

Storms never bothered You, Lord. They were only opportunities to give God glory. In the midst of raging waves, when the spray of salt has drenched all hope of escape, You are still there. Your tranquility speaks peace to my soul.

SIMPLE TRUTH

If God had intended for us to swim on our own, He
would not have given us a lifeboat.

SOWER

"The one who
sowed the good seed is
the Son of Man."

MATTHEW 13:37

FROM THE FATHER'S HEART

My child, every good seed that has been planted in your heart comes from Me. I grow wonderful gardens, but the soil must be prepared. I'll help you keep your heart pliable, free of hard clumps. I'll provide the nourishment, but you must provide the soil. I need you to sit in My presence often. Soak up My showers of goodness; drink in My fertilizing love. You need ample doses of the Son in your life. Before you know it, you'll see new growth—and new plants.

A GRATEFUL RESPONSE

You planted me, just like a seed, and from my earliest beginnings, You've watered, fed, and nourished me until I could reproduce other plants. I thank You, Lord, for being the sower of good seed in my life. My eyes are on the Son.

SIMPLE TRUTH

God adorns each day with bouquets of blessings.

BLESSED POTENTATE

*Which in his times he shall shew,
who is the blessed and only Potentate,
the King of kings, and Lord of lords.*

1 TIMOTHY 6:15 KJV

FROM THE FATHER'S HEART

My child, so many think they control their own destinies. Consequently, they attribute every ounce of strength, leadership ability, and wealth to their own efforts. One day, all will see and know where power truly originates—that every good thing comes from My Father. One day all will declare that I am the blessed and only Potentate, the King of kings and Lord of lords. And only those who know Me will have eternal access to My presence.

A GRATEFUL RESPONSE

The lust for power, the hunger of greed, and the exalting of self will one day be destroyed at Your appearing. You are the blessed Potentate, the King of kings, and Lord of lords. You rule and reign within my heart. Lord, may that ever be true.

SIMPLE TRUTH

No word can express, and no tongue can confess adequately, the glory and majesty of God.

AUTHORITY

To the only God our Savior be glory,
majesty, power and authority,
through Jesus Christ our Lord.

JUDE 25

FROM THE FATHER'S HEART

My child, My intimate relationship with you does not preclude the need to respect My authority and leadership in your life. Without it, your life would be like a ship on a storm-tossed sea. Keep following My commands. They will keep you on the right track. And if anyone questions your beliefs, tell them about Me. I am the only real authority that brings freedom.

A GRATEFUL RESPONSE

Lord, even nature waits in hibernation, resting in Your care and listening for Your voice so it can rise once again. Your voice has authority, more than any teacher or ruler who ever lived. I join all of Your creation in honoring You and Your authority.

SIMPLE TRUTH

Some of us are confused. Instead of letting Christ be
Lord over us, we think we are to lord it over others.

SUN OF RIGHTEOUSNESS WITH HEALING IN ITS WINGS

*"But for you who revere my name,
the sun of righteousness will rise with healing in its wings."*

MALACHI 4:2

FROM THE FATHER'S HEART

My child, in this life you will experience injustice, illness, rejection, misunderstanding, and death. But the time is coming when I, the sun of righteousness, will both rise and descend to call My children home. Heaven's healing waits for those who have known and revered Me—and a special place in My kingdom. Don't be weary doing good things in My name. Because you have acknowledged My name, I will acknowledge yours.

A GRATEFUL RESPONSE

One day I'll discard all my worn bandages and frayed Band-Aids—and receive no more doctor bills. You are the sun of righteousness, Lord. Like an eagle soaring in the sky, You'll rise with ultimate healing in Your wings. I'm waiting for that day, Lord.

SIMPLE TRUTH

The Lord delights in those who delight in Him.

Day 341

SHINING LIGHT

As he neared Damascus on his journey,
suddenly a light from heaven flashed around him.

Acts 9:3

From the Father's Heart

My child, I deal with each person differently. Paul needed a
drastic change to turn from his life of persecuting My people. He needed a special anointing for the work I would give
him to do. Later, as he was imprisoned, My light that once
blinded him gave him sight in a dark prison. I am your shining light, too. Never hide your light under a box, thinking
it's unimportant. Let it shine. Let it shine for Me.

A Grateful Response

While walking in darkness, I, too, saw the light. No, not a
blinding light like Paul experienced on the road to Damascus, but a life-changing brilliance. You are that shining
light, Lord. Without Your intervention, my eyes would be
permanently blind. You changed my life forever.

Simple Truth

God calls each of us to light for another the flame once
extinguished by despair.

ASSURANCE

"If you have faith as small as a mustard seed. . . .
Nothing will be impossible for you."

MATTHEW 17:20

FROM THE FATHER'S HEART

My child, do you still have difficulty believing anything is possible? The older you grow, the more you will have to work to see with childlike eyes of faith. A mustard seed is a tiny amount of seed-faith, but it grows into a huge shade tree. My assurance comes from My Father, whose word is all I need. Is My word good enough for you?

A GRATEFUL RESPONSE

Lord, You loved the word *impossible*. No problem was too difficult for You to solve. No person was too diseased for You to heal. No life was too sinful for You to forgive. You placed Your assurance in Your heavenly Father's power, and He never failed to deliver.

SIMPLE TRUTH

A tiny grain of faith will bring a mountain full of hope.

FRIEND WHO STICKS CLOSER THAN A BROTHER

But there is a friend who sticks closer than a brother.

PROVERBS 18:24

FROM THE FATHER'S HEART

My child, I know what it's like to be betrayed by a best friend. One of My close disciples, Judas Iscariot, turned Me over to My enemies for thirty pieces of silver. And all My disciples left Me in My time of deepest need. But I am not like that. I am your best and closest friend for life. You will never regret our friendship. Have I ever let you down?

A GRATEFUL RESPONSE

The best of earthly friends will fail us at times. Even the closest family member will disappoint. But You are the friend who sticks closer than a brother. You are the One who loves me unconditionally. You are the One who never leaves. You are my friend for all seasons.

SIMPLE TRUTH

Jesus is the only One who will lift you up—and never let you down.

ONE APPOINTED BY GOD

*He was faithful to the one who appointed him,
just as Moses was faithful in all God's house.*

HEBREWS 3:2

FROM THE FATHER'S HEART

My child, I did not come to earth on My own authority; nor
did I make My own rules. I was appointed by God to carry
out His will—and that became My meat, My main desire
and purpose, while I lived on earth. Moses, Joshua, and many
others faithfully completed the jobs My Father gave to them.
I expect no less from you. My Father has appointed you for a
purpose, and I live in your heart to help you carry it out.
Everything you do is to bring Him glory.

A GRATEFUL RESPONSE

When you said, "God told Me," or "God spoke to Me," You
were telling the truth. You were not following some man-
made orders; You were the One appointed by God Himself.
You were God's ambassador to the world, and Your good-
will included me. Thank You, Lord.

SIMPLE TRUTH

*The Lord needs your heart—the world needs your
love.*

LONG-SUFFERING

The LORD is longsuffering, and of great mercy,
forgiving iniquity and transgression.

NUMBERS 14:18 KJV

FROM THE FATHER'S HEART

My child, sometimes you are so impatient with your own and others' faults. I know it takes a lifetime to build strong character, and I know My timetable for you. Know that I am long-suffering. My patience never runs out for My children. I am the God of many chances. But remember, the longer you stay away, the harder it is to return. Don't let a single day go by without our fellowship. And while you're at it, be patient with yourself and others. My goodness leads others to repentance, just like My discipline.

A GRATEFUL RESPONSE

Lord, You are long-suffering, slow to get angry or impatient over my faults. You never excuse my sin, but You forgive much more than seventy times seven. Your patience waters my life with fragrant drops, merciful gifts to a dry and parched spirit.

SIMPLE TRUTH

Never demand from others what you are not willing
to give yourself.

ROOT AND OFFSPRING OF DAVID

"I am the Root and the Offspring of David."

REVELATION 22:16

FROM THE FATHER'S HEART

My child, have you taken a look lately at all the names on My family tree? The branches are full of ordinary people like you who dared to be extraordinary for Me. I am the Root and Offspring of David, an ordinary shepherd boy with royalty in his blood. You, My child, are part of that royal family, too. My Spirit flows through every branch. Welcome to My kingdom. Welcome to My heart.

A GRATEFUL RESPONSE

Lord, how precious to know that I've been grafted into Your family tree, dating back even to King David! You are the Root and Offspring of David, and I am only a servant in Your kingdom. But You have made me an heir to the throne. I worship You, Lord.

SIMPLE TRUTH

When God starts His Spirit flowing, there's no telling where it's going.

ONE GREATER THAN THE TEMPLE

"I tell you that one greater than the temple is here."

MATTHEW 12:6

FROM THE FATHER'S HEART

My child, remember that the form may change, but the message never will. Those who are tied to rules, rituals, and age-old traditions fail to see that I am the One greater than the temple. Others still try to appease Me with sacrifices, and in their ignorance, they end up condemning the innocent victim of their schemes. Enlarge your view of who I am. Don't box Me in.

A GRATEFUL RESPONSE

Lord, the tabernacle, the temple, and the law were only pictures of something greater to come. Although prophets had foretold Your coming for years, some totally misunderstood Your purpose. You are the One greater than the temple, a clear picture of the Father.

SIMPLE TRUTH

Earthly temples are built with human hands, but only God can build a spiritual home in our hearts.

RESOURCEFULNESS

Taking the five loaves and the two fish
and looking up to heaven,
he gave thanks and broke the loaves.

MATTHEW 14:19

FROM THE FATHER'S HEART

My child, what's in your hand? When I once asked Moses, I turned his rod to a serpent and back again. I once asked that question of a little boy and multiplied his offering of five loaves and two fish to feed over five thousand men and their families. Whatever you have in your hand is what I will take and use, My child, to feed others and to multiply My kingdom's work. Trust My resourcefulness. What seems little to you is all I need.

A GRATEFUL RESPONSE

Lord, You took a lump of clay and created man. You turn a desert into a springtime garden and dig a well from a mirage. You feed thousands with only crumbs. My "I think I can't" turns to "I know I can" when I look at Your resourcefulness, Lord. You're amazing.

SIMPLE TRUTH

A king deserves a royal prize, beyond all earthly mea-
sure, I'll give my heart, and nothing less—the highest
of my treasure.

REVEALER OF MYSTERIES

*"As you were lying there, O king,
your mind turned to things to come,
and the revealer of mysteries showed you
what is going to happen."*

DANIEL 2:29

FROM THE FATHER'S HEART

My child, life is really simple. You live. You die. You spend eternity with Me. But what mysteries live in between those three events! I am the revealer of mysteries, but I will give you only what you can handle right now. Too much knowledge is a temptation to use for selfish or prideful purposes. Like My servant Daniel, you must give credit to Me when I entrust you with the secrets of My kingdom. He claimed no great wisdom—only servanthood. You, too, are here to bring Me glory, and to help others understand My mysteries.

A GRATEFUL RESPONSE

The foolish hole up in ivory palaces and wait for the world to end, believing they know the date. Others predict, with ungrounded confidence, the day of Your return. But You are the only revealer of mysteries, Lord. You alone, hold the secret of the ages. I look to You as my source.

SIMPLE TRUTH

Life's most difficult problems can only be solved with God.

SUPPLIER OF NEEDS

But my God shall supply all your need according to his riches in glory by Christ Jesus.

PHILIPPIANS 4:19 KJV

FROM THE FATHER'S HEART

My child, have you been begging for crumbs lately? I've prepared steak and potatoes for you, only part of a complete five-course meal. Do you think others will believe I can supply their needs if you don't believe Me? When your heart's desire is to please Me, your requests will be My desires for you. I own it all, My child. Let Me give you some of your inheritance. Let Me supply your needs.

A GRATEFUL RESPONSE

Even when my bank account registers zero, my heart is full of Your provision, Lord. You are the supplier of my need, but not the gratifier of my wants. You are my only true resource. Thank You, Lord, for Your goodness to me.

SIMPLE TRUTH

He invites us to feast at the King's own table, where He has prepared a royal dining place.

SHELTER FROM THE STORM

You have been a refuge for the poor. . .
a shelter from the storm.

ISAIAH 25:4

FROM THE FATHER'S HEART

My child, a storm spells different things to different people. Whether it's a job loss, a shattered reputation, a sick child, or a bankruptcy, I am a shelter from the storm. Any panic you feel isn't caused by what you're going through. Those emotions stem from what you believe—precisely what you believe about Me and My capabilities. Do you believe I'm able to help? Will you let Me hide you from the storm?

A GRATEFUL RESPONSE

You're the cavern by the ocean; You're the lighthouse on the sea. You're the towering oak with leafy arms; You're the cabin in the woods. Wherever danger lurks; wherever winds blow, You are my shelter from the storm. I can hide in You, Lord, until the storm has passed.

SIMPLE TRUTH

Faith is holding on to God's dreams—and letting go
of your own.

BREATH OF THE ALMIGHTY

But it is the spirit in a man,
the breath of the Almighty,
that gives him understanding.

JOB 32:8

FROM THE FATHER'S HEART

My child, apart from Me, you have no wisdom, and life serves no purpose. My Spirit, the breath of the Almighty, blows through your heart, soul, and mind, and fills it with heaven's thoughts and desires. Every time a positive thought is born; each time your heart swells in love toward another; whenever you experience an "aha!" moment of truth; the breath of the Almighty has been at work. It is My Spirit that draws you into My very presence.

A GRATEFUL RESPONSE

Your Spirit is the breath of the Almighty, the One who gives me life, the One who determines my purpose here, the One who helps me understand spiritual truths. You fill up my God-shaped vacuum, Lord. Thank You for breathing on me, Holy Spirit.

SIMPLE TRUTH

Sweet breath comes from putting His words into our mouths.

THE WAY

Thomas said to him,
"Lord, we don't know where you are going,
so how can we know the way?"
Jesus answered, "I am the way."

JOHN 14: 5–6

FROM THE FATHER'S HEART

My child, have you lost your way again? Do you sometimes feel like a three-year-old child standing in a huge shopping mall alone, separated from its mother? When life confuses you, and you don't know which way to turn, run home to Me. I hear your cries. You may wander away. But I never will. I am the way. Follow My footprints, and you'll never lose your way home.

A GRATEFUL RESPONSE

You are my bridge over troubled waters, the path to light my feet. Without You in my life, I have no direction, Lord. I depend on You for my road map of life. You not only show me the way. You are the way.

SIMPLE TRUTH

Jesus—don't leave life without Him.

REVERENCE

Therefore strong peoples will honor you;
cities of ruthless nations will revere you.

ISAIAH 25:3

FROM THE FATHER'S HEART

My child, in the same way that I revere My Father, I enjoy when you reverence My Father. And I enjoy when you reverence My name. When you speak the name of Jesus softly, like an adoring child, My arms open wide to receive you. And when you shout My name boldly in the presence of the enemy, I send heaven's host rushing to your defense. Know that when you bow at My feet and offer tears of gratitude and repentance, My love engulfs you and receives your praises gladly. These are holy moments to Me.

A GRATEFUL RESPONSE

Even Your enemies hush when heaven speaks Your name. All creation bows with wonder as the night of miracles approaches. You revered Your Father, always doing what honored Him the most. I, too, bow in reverence and celebrate Your coming, Lord.

SIMPLE TRUTH

There are times when a holy God desires a holy hush
in His presence.

PRINCE OF PEACE

For to us a child is born. . . .
And he will be called. . .Prince of Peace.

ISAIAH 9:6

FROM THE FATHER'S HEART

My child, how the world longs for peace! Just as I wept over My beloved Jerusalem and My people's rejection of Me, I mourn when men and women today look for peace—in everything but Me. As Prince of Peace, I was born not to rule government, but to rule and bring peace to hearts everywhere. I love when you look to Me for peace, My child. I give you My peace—peace with God and the peace of God, both found in Me.

A GRATEFUL RESPONSE

Your arrival brought great promise: peace to all the world. Some came seeking an end to oppression; others expected a prince to rule. As Prince of Peace, You brought the only lasting peace—not with the world, but with God. And You came to rule in the heart, not on an earthly throne. Thank You for Your peace, Lord.

SIMPLE TRUTH

When Jesus entered the world, peace entered our hearts.

ONE BORN OF GOD

We know that anyone born of God does not continue to sin;
the one who was born of God keeps him safe,
and the evil one cannot harm him.

1 JOHN 5:18

FROM THE FATHER'S HEART

My child, those called by My name don't make a habit of
disobedience. I am the One born of God, and you are born
of Me. You don't have to take in boarders when trouble and
temptation stalk the rooms of your heart. When they show
up, tell them you're closed—for renovations. I will take care
of those who want to harm you. Though others may try to
hurt your body and mind, your spirit is safe forever.

A GRATEFUL RESPONSE

You are God's miracle to us, the One born of God. Because
of who You are, I can hide in the safety of Your arms, knowing that You will protect me from harm. Because of whose
I am, I can rejoice in the knowledge that I am loved and celebrate Christmas every day.

SIMPLE TRUTH

When a door opens, make sure it is God who opens it.

STAR

When they saw the star,
they were overjoyed.

MATTHEW 2:10

FROM THE FATHER'S HEART

My child, search for Me daily with as much diligence as the wise men on the night of My birth. My "star" still shines. I still bring hope. I continue to light the way for anyone who seeks to worship Me. And as long as you keep Me on the throne of your life, you won't have to look far to find Me.

A GRATEFUL RESPONSE

In search of the star, I journey far to see my heart's delight. There, all along, in the day or the night, You wait to receive my gifts of praise and adoration. I have seen the light; I have found love wrapped in a manger. You, Lord, will always be the star of my life.

SIMPLE TRUTH

At the center of Christmas is the heart of God.

BORN OF A VIRGIN

*"The virgin will be with child
and will give birth to a son."*

MATTHEW 1:23

FROM THE FATHER'S HEART
My child, some still can't believe My supernatural birth. How I long for them to mirror Mary's attitude, one not of disbelief, but of wonder: "How can this be?" she asked in awe, yet she surrendered her total heart, mind, and body to My Father: "May it be to me as you have said." I was born of a virgin, not a super-saint, just an ordinary woman with extraordinary faith and humility. It's that same spirit I want for all My children, including you, My child. I desire to do extraordinary things through you.

A GRATEFUL RESPONSE
Lord, what a wonder that You were born of a virgin, conceived by the Holy Spirit, and sealed with heaven's kiss. The purest sacrifice, the sweetest gift, God's own child—You are truly a miracle. I celebrate You, Lord.

SIMPLE TRUTH
Impossibilities are God's specialties.

BETHLEHEM'S BABE

"Let's go to Bethlehem. . . ."
So they hurried off and found Mary and Joseph,
and the baby, who was lying in the manger.

LUKE 2:15–16

FROM THE FATHER'S HEART

My child, what a pity that I am still a babe in arms to so many. I was the prophesied babe born in the quiet, humble town of Bethlehem. Angels announced Me, and kings and shepherds revered me. Many still portray Me in a manger. I am no longer a baby, yet some refuse to make Me Lord in their hearts, to acknowledge that Bethlehem's babe is the Son of God who now sits at the right hand of the Father. Will you complete for them the rest of the story?

A GRATEFUL RESPONSE

Long ago, You looked down and gave the world its most prized possession. Bethlehem's babe, Jesus, born in a manger— what a humble, yet extraordinary beginning! Lord, my heart will be Your Bethlehem, where You can place Your throne. You're welcome in my home anytime.

SIMPLE TRUTH
Jesus makes room in our hearts for love.

GIFT OF GOD

*"If you knew the gift of God
and who it is that asks you. . . ."*

JOHN 4:10

FROM THE FATHER'S HEART

My child, of all the gifts you receive this year, what can compare to the very first gift—Jesus? Which one offers lasting peace and eternal security? After the ribbons are torn from their brightly wrapped boxes, which ones will bring contentment and comfort and hope long after the celebrations are past? My child, keep Me in your celebrations—always. And remember to celebrate with childlike faith My greatest gift to you for all time.

A GRATEFUL RESPONSE

You are more precious than incense, more costly than gold, more fragrant than myrrh—You are the priceless gift of God. I can only offer You humble gifts—a solitary prayer, a sacrifice of gratitude and praise, a broken life. Jesus, You'll always be the very best gift to me.

SIMPLE TRUTH

Jesus is the only gift that lasts forever.

IMMANUEL, GOD WITH US

"And they will call him Immanuel"
—which means, "God with us."

MATTHEW 1:23

FROM THE FATHER'S HEART

My child, in between the miracles and celebrations of life are the most difficult times for you to remember Me. Mountaintop moments bring just that—moments of My glory that I allow as a sneak preview of things to come. But what goes up must come down. In the valleys and as you walk through ordinary days, My power is still yours for the asking and receiving. I am Immanuel, God with us. And I am with you day in and day out—forever.

A GRATEFUL RESPONSE

You are Immanuel, God with us, daily. You no longer live in columns of clouds or pillars of fire. Your home is not confined to the walls of a tabernacle, church, or temple. You are not just a babe of Bethlehem. Thank You, Lord, that You now live in my heart.

SIMPLE TRUTH

Others listen more closely when you're in the valley than they do when you're on the mountaintop.

VISION

*For he chose us in him before the creation of the world
to be holy and blameless in his sight.*

EPHESIANS 1:4

FROM THE FATHER'S HEART

My child, do you still wonder about why or where I've placed you on this earth? Do you question My intentions—or My work in your life? Perhaps it is because you don't yet share My vision. Behind the scenes I am working out all the details of My world—and how you fit into it—so you can know, like Esther, that you were here "for such a time as this." Be patient, My child. Catch My vision. Follow Me daily, and you'll see a glorious future unfold.

A GRATEFUL RESPONSE

Long before we entered the scene, before You ever revealed Your plan for creation, You chose us to shine and give praise to You, Lord. In the beginning, before we were ever born, You adopted us as Your own. Even when I'm clueless, Lord, I trust You. You know what You're doing. You are truly a God of vision.

SIMPLE TRUTH

*We hope, dream, and make our plans, but the future
belongs in God's hands.*

MOST HOLY PLACE

*Behind the second curtain was a room called
the Most Holy Place.*

HEBREWS 9:3

FROM THE FATHER'S HEART

My child, just as My high priests in Scripture enjoyed
sacred moments in the Most Holy Place, I treasure our time
together daily. You are free to come and go as you wish. No
curtains separate us now. Only sin can break the fellowship,
but your sonship is forever. Guard our time, My child. I am
your Most Holy Place now. I deserve the best, and I want
all of you—mind, body, and spirit. I want to know that you
and your heart are really "there" with Me.

A GRATEFUL RESPONSE

In that quiet spot each morning, Lord, where I come to share
my heart, You wait expectantly. You are the Most Holy Place,
a sacred dwelling place now open for all to enter. Thank You
for tearing the curtain down, the past barrier to our fellowship. Thank You for inviting me into Your presence. Lord, if
You gave me access to Your most private room, surely I can
entrust the keys to the rooms of my heart to You—including
all the secret places.

SIMPLE TRUTH

Children love to hear the sound of their Father's voice.

ETERNAL LIFE

*He is the true God
and eternal life.*

1 JOHN 5:20

FROM THE FATHER'S HEART

My child, eternal life begins not just when you step across death's threshold, but rather, the moment you let Me step into your heart forever. I am eternal life. I am your forever hope. When your physical body finally says goodbye, and you walk into your new heavenly body, you will experience in full measure the taste of joy you had while on earth. No more sorrow, no more tears. If you know Me, you have eternal life.

A GRATEFUL RESPONSE

Some say life begins at forty, while others believe eighteen is the magic age. (Some senior citizens will argue for sixty-five!) But real life, eternal life, began for me the moment You entered my heart years ago. Lord, You are eternal life. You are my home forever.

SIMPLE TRUTH

Life begins with Jesus.

FORGETFULNESS

"For I will forgive their wickedness
and will remember their sins no more."

HEBREWS 8:12

FROM THE FATHER'S HEART

My child, why are you digging up old behaviors for Me to forgive? Was My word not enough the first time? My victory on the cross paid for every sin you will ever commit. I will never tolerate new sin behaviors. I will empower you to live in your new nature. But My forgetfulness is to your advantage. It means I no longer record sin to your account. When I clean out the rooms of your heart, I will fill them with beautiful new furnishings—things that are worthy of a child of God.

A GRATEFUL RESPONSE

Lord, parts of my past are like stains on the artist's palette. But with one stroke of Your brush, You blend all the colors to form a beautiful masterpiece. What I remember, You erase. Lord, thank You for Your forgetfulness—for remembering to forget.

SIMPLE TRUTH
What God forgives, God forgets.

THE AMEN

"These are the words of the Amen."

REVELATION 3:14

FROM THE FATHER'S HEART

My child, another day has come and gone, perhaps another month or year or season in your life. But through it all, I have been the Amen: the source of creation and comfort and blessing; the giver of good and praiseworthy and beautiful in you; the benediction to every plan and purpose I've designed. I am where life, real life, begins and ends. I am the One who blesses and encourages you, and who will one day announce as you stand before My throne in heaven, "Well done, My child! Amen! So be it! Your reward awaits you."

A GRATEFUL RESPONSE

You are the sunrise of every morning, the perfect Amen to every night. Throughout the day, I watch in amazement as You work out Your will and Your ways. Though my vision is limited, my heart joins creation in a chorus of praise to a magnificent God: "Amen, Lord. So be it."

SIMPLE TRUTH

*No words can comfort like the ones from the Father's
 heart.*

IN YOUR PRESENCE

Perhaps you have never come to know the personal and intimate presence of God in your life. If He has placed such a desire in your heart, may I share with you some simple steps so you can become acquainted with the Father personally?

1. Admit the sin in your life and the need in your heart for God (Romans 3:23).

2. Acknowledge that Jesus loves you and that He died for your sin (John 3:16).

3. Ask Jesus to forgive you, to come into your life, and to fill you with His personal, intimate presence (Revelation 3:20).

4. By faith, thank Him that you are now His child, and confess that from now on, He will be the Lord and Love of your life. Give Him the key to all the rooms of your heart (Romans 10:9–10, John 1:12).

If I can help your Christian growth in any way, please let me know.

ABOUT THE AUTHOR

Rebecca Barlow Jordan writes from her home in Greenville, Texas.

———❧———

If this book has encouraged you in any way, Rebecca would love to hear from you.

She is also available for speaking engagements. You may contact her at:

P.O. Box 8323
Greenville, TX 75404–8323

or by contacting

Speak Up Speaker Services
Toll free at (888) 870-7719 or at the following E-mail address: Speakupinc@aol.com

For more information, see Rebecca's Web site at:
www.rebeccabarlowjordan.com

Inspirational Library

Beautiful purse/pocket-size editions of Christian classics bound in flexible leatherette. These books make thoughtful gifts for everyone on your list, including yourself!

When I'm on My Knees   The highly popular collection of devotional thoughts on prayer, especially for women.
>   Flexible Leatherette. $4.97

The Bible Promise Book   Over 1,000 promises from God's Word arranged by topic. What does God promise about matters like: Anger, Illness, Jealousy, Love, Money, Old Age, and Mercy? Find out in this book!
>   Flexible Leatherette. $3.97

Daily Wisdom for Women   A daily devotional for women seeking biblical wisdom to apply to their lives. Scripture taken from the New American Standard Version of the Bible.
>   Flexible Leatherette. $5.97

A Gentle Spirit   With an emphasis on personal spiritual development, this daily devotional for women draws from the best writings of Christian female authors.
>   Flexible Leatherette. $5.97

Available wherever books are sold.
Or order from:

Barbour Publishing, Inc.
P.O. Box 719
Uhrichsville, OH 44683
www.barbourbooks.com

If you order by mail, add $2.00 to your order for shipping.
Prices are subject to change without notice.